Understanding Special Education

Understanding Special Education

An Examination of the Responsibilities through Case Studies

Roberta Gentry and Norah S. Hooper

ROWMAN & LITTLEFIELD
Lanham • Boulder • New York • London

Published by Rowman & Littlefield
A wholly owned subsidiary of The Rowman & Littlefield Publishing Group, Inc.
4501 Forbes Boulevard, Suite 200, Lanham, Maryland 20706
www.rowman.com

Unit A, Whitacre Mews, 26-34 Stannary Street, London SE11 4AB

British Library Cataloguing in Publication Information Available

Library of Congress Cataloging-in-Publication Data

Names: Gentry, Roberta, author. | Hooper, Norah S., author.
Title: Understanding special education : an examination of the responsibilities through case studies / Roberta Gentry and Norah S. Hooper.
Description:: Lanham : Rowman & Littlefield, [2016] | Includes bibliographical references and index.
Identifiers: : LCCN 2016010415 (print) | LCCN 2016012569 (ebook) | ISBN 9781475822175 (cloth : alk. paper) | ISBN 9781475822205 (pbk. : alk. paper) | ISBN 9781475822212 (Electronic)
Subjects: : LCSH: Special education--United States--Case studies.
Classification:: LCC LC3981 .G45 2016 (print) | LCC LC3981 (ebook) | DDC 371.9--dc23 LC record available at http://lccn.loc.gov/2016010415

Printed in the United States of America

Contents

Foreword   vii

Introduction   ix

1   The Pre-Referral Process and Response to Intervention   1
     Response to Intervention   3
     Case 1: Interventions for Whom?   4
     Case 2: Are More Intensive Interventions Warranted?   6

2   Eligibility for Special Education Services   9
     Case 3: What Should the Team Decide?   11
     Case 4: What Are the Next Steps?   14

3   Individualized Education Program   17
     Case 5: Is the School Providing Appropriate Services?   19
     Case 6: What Should Tommy Do Next Year?   22

4   Working with Parents   25
     Families in Crisis   25
     From a Parent's View   26
     Resources for Parents   27
     Advocacy   28
     The Reality of Parenting a Child with a Disability   29
     A Valuable Resource   31
     Case 7: What Can Parents Do?   31
     Case 8: Who Is Responsible?   34

5   Co-Teaching   39
     One Teach, One Observe   39
     One Teach, One Assist   40
     Station Teaching   40
     Parallel Teaching   40
     Alternative Teaching   40
     Team Teaching   41
     Case 9: Will They Co-Teach?   42
     Case 10: What Should Mr. Walker Do?   45

6   Working with Other Professionals   49
     Related Services   50
     Speech and Language Services   51
     Occupational Therapist   51

Physical Therapy — 52
Other Professionals — 53
Teaming — 54
Case 11: Where Is the Team? — 56
Case 12: Should Evelyn Have Come Home? — 60

7   The Effective Classroom — 65
Create a Classroom Community — 65
Use Space Thoughtfully — 66
Develop Routines — 67
Anticipate Problems — 67
Use Prompts — 68
Teach School Behavior — 69
Hold Everyone Accountable — 70
Be Persistent — 71
Case 13: What Does an Effective Classroom Look Like? — 71
Connections — 72
Independence — 72
Responsibility and Choice — 73
Frequent Assessment — 74
Variety — 74
Case 14: Does Rodney Have a Disability? — 75

8   Behavior Management — 79
Foundation — 79
Bernie — 79
Manifestation Determination — 80
Case 15: Where Does Billy Belong? — 85
Case 16: Can Michael Control Himself? — 89

9   Assessment — 93
Definition — 93
Classroom Data Collection — 95
Test Accessibility — 99
Test Accommodations — 99
Alternate Assessment — 101
Case 17: How Can Assessment Help Marcus? — 103
Case 18: Is This Test Fair? — 106

Appendix A: List of Cases by Disability Area — 109
Appendix B: List of Cases by Grade Level — 111
References — 113
About the Authors — 115

Foreword

I have been involved in the preparation of teachers of students with and without disabilities for more than eighteen years and know how important it is to not only teach methods and strategies, but to also help students understand that context matters as well. For teachers working on completing an initial licensure program, they may not have enough classroom experience to draw on to make lecture-based discussions sufficient. That's where the use of case studies is particularly helpful and why I was so pleased to review the plans for this book, and to see the care with which the authors have organized the content and structure used for the book as a whole and the integration of the case studies in particular.

Authors Roberta Gentry and Norah Hooper draw on their own classroom experiences to bring this book and the cases included in each chapter alive. Like many introductory books designed as an overview of the field of special education for general education teachers, it covers the range of topics needed to successfully provide meaningful access to the general education curriculum for students with disabilities.

While the authors provide information about how specific disabilities can impact a student's ability to learn, they do not stop there. Instead, each chapter focuses on specific strategies and methods, providing an overview of the topic, descriptions of Evidence-Based Practices, and then uses one or more case studies to provide contextual information about how it can be used with a specific student or how the strategy can be implemented in a real world setting. Additionally, the role of the general education teacher is highlighted in each of the case studies, which is a welcome addition to the case study design; not only does it provide a concrete example, it specifically provides guidance for the general education teacher (or teacher to be).

I look forward to using this book to supplement the coursework offered by our department for students in our university's programs in teaching and learning. It is destined to be a staple in such programs across the country.

Colleen A. Thoma, Professor and Chair
Departments of Counselor Education and Special Education and
Disability Policy, Virginia Commonwealth University

Introduction

Real life is messy. School life is especially messy, with the individual personalities of students, teachers, parents, and administrators interacting in unexpected ways. Prospective teachers may have a good grasp of teaching techniques and relevant legal information but still have no idea how to act when they are on the job. The messiness is not reflected in textbook narratives or lists or even in short vignettes depicting successful teachers.

Case studies can capture that messiness. They tell a real story, raise thorny issues, depict the motivations of characters in conflict, portray actors in moments of decision, and leave the reader with no clear-cut right answers. As they process the cases in this book, participants will learn to collect and evaluate data, identify important concepts, apply legal requirements, develop hypotheses, and create or defend arguments (McKeachie, 1999).

In increasing numbers, general education teachers are faced with the task of educating students with disabilities in their classrooms. The cases in this book are written from the viewpoint of general education teachers, with the goal of providing teachers with the information and tools to improve their ability to approach this task with confidence. For example, the chapter on "Working with Other Professionals" will inform them of the roles these professionals play in the education of the students and will also help them gain collaborative skills.

Most special education books are organized by the various disabilities. However, current inclusion practices have led to classrooms that serve students with several different disabilities. In addition, many issues are not particular to single disabilities. Therefore, this book is organized by special education topics such as co-teaching, working with parents, and assessment. Regardless of the disability, these topics will be relevant to all teachers. The cases move beyond particular disabilities, including complicated scenarios that are typical in school settings. A chart of cases by disability is included in appendix A and by grade level in appendix B.

Each chapter begins with a section giving basic information about the topic. Readers learn about laws related to discipline of students with disabilities, successful co-teaching practices, and classroom practices that help students with disabilities succeed. They can then apply this information to their analysis of the two cases presented in the chapter. The questions and activities that follow each case are intended to help the readers understand what is happening in the situation and extend their understanding through reflection and further research.

This collection of cases is designed to be used in one of two ways:

1. They can be used in an introductory special education graduate or undergraduate course. It may be either the initial course in a special education teacher preparation program or a special education course taken by students planning to become general education teachers. The cases may be most successfully used as a supplement to a comprehensive textbook.

2. Another appropriate use would be as a focus of a professional development activity for inservice teachers. Since each of the cases is told from the point of view of a general education teacher, they will provide a lens through which practicing teachers can learn about disability characteristics and legal requirements, and can reflect on their own practice. It might also be useful to select single chapters to serve specific purposes, such helping teachers deal with a thorny situation in their school.

The cases are based on real-life situations that general education teachers are likely to face in their classrooms. Some of them present ideal practices and attitudes that lead to successful outcomes, while others depict troublesome mistakes made by teachers and others. Through their analysis of the issues presented in the cases, both future and practicing teachers can become better prepared to address the needs of students with disabilities in their own classrooms.

The successful use of case studies requires close instructor supervision, particularly at the beginning. Because students are often used to having one correct answer, the process of examining real-life situations and coming to some conclusions about possible actions can be an unfamiliar one.

1. As an instructor, determine why you are using a particular case and what information, understandings, or procedures you expect the participants to gain from the experience.

2. Establish participation ground rules. Emphasize open discussion with all questions welcome, procedures for speaking in turn, and the importance of collaboration in reaching a thorough analysis of the issues presented.

3. Use a procedure to ensure that each participant has read the case before coming to the group session. Requiring a short written summary is one way, as is calling on someone randomly to summarize the case orally. It is also helpful to have students attempt to answer some of the discussion questions before the session, although no penalty should be imposed for "incorrect" answers. The point is to

have them wrestle with the issues on their own so they make a meaningful contribution to the discussion.

4. There are numerous ways to do the initial work on the cases as a group. The method chosen can vary from case to case depending on the issues posed, or from group to group depending on the experiences and dynamics of the participants. Some possibilities are:

   a. Assign a student or pair of students to prepare a presentation of the case to the class. This group will summarize the issues, present relevant legal and court information, relate the issues to school policies and practices, and so on. Another part of their presentation will be to involve the group in an activity that helps them to understand the essential elements of the case. They could use one of the suggested activities in the book or develop an activity of their own.

   b. After a general discussion of the important elements of the case, assign a character in the case to each of the participants. It becomes the responsibility of each person to "get inside" the character, understanding their experiences, motivations, and feelings. They then act out selected events of the case (such as an Individualized Education Program [IEP] meeting) in which the characters' viewpoints are aired.

   c. Establish permanent case discussion groups at the beginning of the semester or professional development seminar. Have each group develop ways to assign roles such as discussion leader, timekeeper, and scribe. This permanent assignment allows the instructor to structure the groups so that they represent varied levels of experience and expertise. Each group discusses the specific elements of the week's case and their implications, answers one or two of the discussion questions, and then presents their conclusions to the larger group.

5. Once the case elements are thoroughly understood by the participants, it is important to move on to the next level. At this point a large group discussion can be held in which the topics are no longer treated as abstract ideas, but become personalized. Questions such as "What would you do in this situation?" "How do your values determine your actions in this situation?" will lead the participants through the process of integrating the case information with their own experiences and understanding which courses of action they should follow in the future. At this point the instructor

may want to use a method to determine how well the participants met the goals set at the beginning. It could be done through additional group discussion or written reflections.

6. Finally, a summarizing discussion is essential. The focus should be not only on the content of the case, but also on the process of evaluation ("Teaching with Case Studies," 1994). The instructor should give feedback on the evaluation process—noting how well the groups worked together, reached important conclusions, and so on. In addition, if some issues remain unclear or incomplete, participants can be assigned the task of researching the topic and bringing the new information to the next session.

The case study methods selected will vary from group to group and possibly case to case. Make full yet judicious use of the websites, questions, and suggested activities. They can be very useful in extending the students' knowledge and compassion. It is important to allot the time required for a full analysis that moves the students to the expected understandings.

A final extension could consist of asking participants to choose one of the topics and write their own case highlighting the important elements. At the end of the course these could be presented to the group for discussion.

ONE

The Pre-Referral Process and Response to Intervention

The general education teacher typically plays a vital role in the pre-referral/referral process. Having spent the most time with the student in an educational setting, they are typically the one bringing the concerns to the committee. These meetings are called a variety of names including Student Support Team, Student Study Team, Student Success Team, Child Study meeting, and Special Education Team meeting.

Regardless of their name, the function is the same; to listen to the concerns, review data, review strategies, or interventions implemented and their outcomes, and to discuss the student who is struggling. These meetings are convened based on academic, behavioral, or social concerns and the meetings are designed for general education students who are not making progress in the curriculum.

In addition to school personnel, parents may initiate these meetings. However, the general education teacher is typically the main conveyer of knowledge and information at the meeting. Furthermore, the outcome of the meeting may vary based on the teacher's information and the data presented, therefore, it is imperative that the teacher comes prepared.

This meeting is different from a parent-teacher conference and it includes members of a multidisciplinary team. This team consists of a general education teacher, a special educator, an administrator, the parents, and, depending on the concerns, other individuals such as a speech language pathologist, a school psychologist, guidance counselor, or an occupational therapist. The administrative, professional, support personnel, and the parents determine if an intervention in the general education setting, or if a referral for special education evaluation, is warranted.

The goal of this problem-solving committee is to listen to the issues presented, review the data provided, and develop recommendations for meeting the student's needs. The team analyzes the student's learning and behavioral characteristics and how these affect access to the curriculum. Also, under consideration are the teaching methods, routines, and procedures that are (or are not) in place in the general education classroom. Pertinent school and home factors are also discussed.

A teacher who is well prepared for these meetings will bring results of classroom assessments, work samples, attendance record, behavior documentation, test results from tests routinely administered within the classroom, progress reports, and report cards. This well prepared teacher will also have documentation of interventions, modifications, and accommodations attempted including the dates and the results of these efforts.

Having compiled this information they will be able to present it in an organized and concise manner, free of educational jargon, in which everyone, including the parents, can understand. Data beyond grades and summative assessments should be provided.

Based on requirements outlined in the Every Student Succeeds act, it is expected that the student have been taught using evidence based researched methods; therefore the methods and materials utilized for instruction may be questioned during the meeting.

The parents are also a vital member of this team and can provide background information on their child's social, emotional, medical, and academic history. Importantly, all members of the team should remember to highlight the student's strengths. All team members contribute and decisions are made at the group level. If a plan is developed to implement, it is important that the general education teacher continue to document the student's response to these interventions and continue to keep data and copious notes to prepare for the follow-up meeting.

Four possible outcomes of this meeting are: (1) continue to monitor the student; (2) develop an Intervention Plan; (3) refer the student for special education services and/or 504 and determine the assessment components that will be completed; or (4) to do nothing if the committee does not suspect a disability. If the team decides to develop a plan for implementation; the team will choose interventions to implement and schedule a follow up meeting to discuss the interventions and outcomes. Follow-up meetings are individualized based on the student's needs and the nature of the plan developed.

At subsequent meetings, individuals review implementation of the plan and the outcomes to determine next steps. Possible outcomes may include creating and implementing a new plan, determining that the plan is working, and deciding if the team needs to meet again, or referring the student for special education evaluation. The team may determine that the student is responding to interventions, to change the interventions, or if a disability is suspected, to refer the student for a special education evaluation. The team may also recommend consideration for a 504 plan.

RESPONSE TO INTERVENTION

Response to Intervention (RTI) is a multi-tier approach to the early identification and support of students with learning and behavior needs (RTI Action Network, 2014). The RTI process begins with high-quality instruction and universal screening of all students in the general education classroom. Struggling learners are provided with interventions at increasing levels of intensity to accelerate their rate of learning. These services may be provided by a variety of personnel, including general education teachers, special educators, and specialists. Progress is closely monitored to assess both the learning rate and level of performance of individual students.

Educational decisions about the intensity and duration of interventions are based on individual student response to instruction. RTI is designed for use when making decisions in both general education and special education, creating a well-integrated system of instruction and intervention guided by child outcome data (RTI Network, 2014). Special education services are designed for students who have a disability and require specialized instruction. While early intervention has provided benefits, it is essential that as a field we do not over identify students for special education services.

Additional Resources:

Below are links to information about RTI:

1. The RTI Action Network provides a general overview of the RTI process, the research behind the process, and behavioral and academic interventions. http://www.rtinetwork.org/learn/what/whatisrti.
2. The RTI Action Network is arranged by the four components of RTI: data based decision making, screening, progress monitoring, and the multilevel system.
3. http://www.rti4success.org/.
4. In addition to academic and behavioral interventions, and videos; Intervention Central provides Curriculum-Based Measurement (CBM) probes. The site can be accessed here: http://www.interventioncentral.org/.
5. The IRIS Site provides four self-paced modules on RTI. The modules can be accessed at this location: http://iris.peabody.vanderbilt.edu/iris-resource-locator/.

Below are resources for the Child Study Process:

1. Newport News Public Schools shared their Pre Child Study and Child Study Handbook here: http://sbo.nn.k12.va.us/sped/documents/child-study-process.pdf.

2. Another example shared by Austin Public Schools is located here: http://www.childstudysystem.com/uploads/6/1/9/1/6191025/child_study_systems_process_manual.pdf.
3. Reasonable accommodations and modifications are discussed here: http://www.greatschools.org/special-education/LD-ADHD/517-pre-referral.gs.
4. A step by step guide to the Child Study Process is provided by Richmond Public Schools: http://web.richmond.k12.va.us/Portals/20/assets/pdfs/AHMSChildStudyProcess2013.pdf.

CASE 1: INTERVENTIONS FOR WHOM?

Mrs. Brown is a sixth grade algebra teacher at Somerset Middle School. This is her third year of teaching Algebra I. The school is located in a lower socio economic section of the city and Mrs. Brown's class consists of Hispanic (50 percent), White (25 percent), African American (18 percent), and Mixed or Other Race (7 percent) students. Two of the students are identified as having disabilities—Caesar has a learning disability and Martin has an emotional disability.

Mrs. Brown and her team of three other algebra teachers, the math specialist, and the special education resource teacher meet regularly to discuss class progress, individual student's progress, and to plan. The team is very knowledgeable regarding the Response to Intervention process and this is the third year the school has implemented this process. They are also aware of Evidence Based Instruction. The team is meeting today to discuss Mrs. Brown's class data.

Mrs. Brown is concerned because her previous classes had scored higher on class assessments. She is using the same materials that she taught with during the last two years, therefore, she does not know why this class is scoring so poorly. She is already considering referring several students for special education. According to Mrs. Brown, these students just don't seem to get it. The table below shows the first two Curriculum-Based Measurement scores for her class:

Questions to Ponder

1. Calculate the mean for each student. Students with means below five are monitored to determine responsiveness to intervention. How many students scored a mean of five or below?
2. Should Mrs. Brown refer these students for Response to Intervention or special education services? Why or Why not?
3. What should Mrs. Brown do next?
4. If you were another teacher on the team, what advice/suggestions would you give Mrs. Brown?

Student	Week 2	Week 3	Mean
Amanda	4	7	
Ariel	10	12	
Anand	2	4	
Charles	4	8	
Ceasar	1	3	
Cynthia	4	8	
Daniel	2	6	
Dominique	4	8	
Emily	2	1	
Emanuel	4	4	
Garrett	2	6	
Helena	4	4	
Irena	4	4	
Jamantha	1	2	
Juries	6	10	
Lionel	2	4	
Martin	1	3	
Michelle	3	5	
Monique	2	5	
Monica	4	6	
Snequa	6	6	
Shatarra	4	2	
Tyler	2	4	
Xavier	6	10	

5. Describe possible interventions or other instructional programs to assist the student's struggling.
6. Mrs. Brown has two students with disabilities in her class, is she required to provide special services to these two students?

Activities to Complete:

1. What Evidence Based Practices should Mrs. Brown use with the class? Support your answer.
2. Create a class graph using Mrs. Brown's class data. Do you recognize any trends in the data?
3. All teachers are required to meet with the principal after initial classroom evaluations are completed, role play the meeting.

CASE 2: ARE MORE INTENSIVE INTERVENTIONS WARRANTED?

Charles is a ninth grade student at Applebee High School in Reading, Pennsylvania. Charles and his mother, Joyce, recently moved to the area from western Kentucky. Charles's father was recently incarcerated and Joyce is struggling financially so she decided to move to her mother's house. She hoped that a move to Pennsylvania would provide a fresh start for Charles, it would reduce her monthly living expenses, and she could help her aging mother. In the small town that they moved from everyone knew that Charles's father was in prison.

Charles is the youngest of three boys. His older brothers have moved out of the family home and are successful. Charles misses his brothers and did not want to move away from them. Initially, Charles had difficulty fitting in at the new school and his mother and teachers assured him that he would adjust quickly, make new friends, and possibly find new interests in Pennsylvania.

Six months after the move, Charles continues to experience difficulties. According to him, everything had been turned upside down in his life and he is angry. He liked his old house, he had friends there, and he misses his brothers. In Kentucky, he used to hunt and fish with his friends, but here, the other kids did not do those things. They were into skateboarding and playing video games and laughed at him when he inquired about hunting and fishing. Charles played some video games, but he enjoyed being outside and especially spending time in the woods walking or hunting.

Furthermore, the students keep teasing him and telling him that he talks funny and keep asking him where he is from. Since the move, Charles has not made any friends. He wants to go back to his old life. He is angry at his mother. He misses his brothers. Why did his mother move here?

Mr. Gallo, Charles's algebra teacher, received his class data from the Algebra Foundations probe, a research based progress monitoring tool. The score indicated that Charles has not shown improvement since the beginning of the year. It is now January and Mr. Gallo, following the Response to Intervention (RTI) guidelines had administered three probes and Charles has not shown growth over the three probes. Meanwhile, his classmates were improving an average of 2.4 correct responses per week.

Mr. Gallo had mentioned Charles previously at the regularly scheduled data meetings and the team had recommended continuing to monitor Charles's progress. After all, he had recently had a lot of changes in his life and was having difficulty adjusting to his new school.

However, at this meeting, they decided to move Charles to small group instruction with the math specialist and change instruction to a program called Cognitive Tutor. This program combines information from the textbook with interactive computer programs. In addition to his regular math time, Charles will work with the math specialist in a small group three times weekly. The team also discussed that this might be a good way to establish friends.

The small group instruction continued for four weeks prior to the next data meeting. Based on the probe, Charles and one other student showed a poor response by scoring only five correct. Other students in the group showed a much more positive response and much higher scores.

Questions to Ponder

1. What indicators were present that showed that Charles had needs beyond the core instruction?
2. How do you know this is not a teacher or school based issue?
3. Do you think Charles's academic issues are related to his difficulties adjusting to the move? Why or why not?
4. Was the core instruction research based? How do you know?
5. What tier is Charles receiving instruction in?
6. What are the next steps?
7. What is your prediction for what will be the outcome at the next data meeting?
8. As a team member at the next data meeting, what questions would you present?
9. When should Charles's mother be notified?

Activities to Complete

1. Prepare for the data meeting. What information will you gather? How will you present the evidence? What are your recommendations for the next steps?
2. Determine if there are other interventions that may be helpful for Charles and the other students struggling. Refer to the What Works Clearinghouse site.
3. Determine if the Cognitive Program was implemented with fidelity.

TWO

Eligibility for Special Education Services

Teachers, other concerned individuals, and parents may refer students for special education services. Referrals may also occur if the student does not make sufficient process utilizing the Response to Intervention approach. Once a referral is received, a school-based interdisciplinary team meets with the parents and determines if an evaluation for special education services is warranted.

The team of qualified professionals includes a special education teacher, a general (regular) education teacher, an individual knowledgeable about the assessment instruments, the child's parents or legal guardian, an administrative representative, an individual knowledgeable about the interpretation of instructional implications of evaluation results, and the child, when appropriate. Other individuals may participate at the discretion of the parents and the school.

Prior to an initial evaluation for special education services, parental consent must be obtained in writing. According to the Individuals with Disabilities Education Act (IDEA), an evaluation must occur prior to provision of special education and related services. IDEA also requires the use of a variety of assessment tools and specifically states that eligibility determination cannot be made based on one instrument. These technically sound assessment instruments must be administered in the child's native language or other mode of communication, by trained and knowledgeable individuals, and in accordance with the instructions provided by the producer of the assessment.

Evaluations are individualized based on the needs of the child and the concerns expressed by the team. The evaluation should be "sufficiently comprehensive to identify all of the child's special education and related service needs" (§ 300.305). The team has sixty days to conduct these eval-

9

uations and must make them available to the parents prior to the meeting to determine eligibility.

At the eligibility meeting, the general education teacher provides grades, the student's academic progress, and other updated information that has occurred since the referral for special education services. Reports are shared from the assessments using language that the parents can understand. The parents provide valuable input. The special education teacher may have only had limited interaction with the student up until this meeting and often does not have new information to share.

From a parent's perspective, these meetings can be incredibly intimidating. Members of the team, other than the parents, tend to speak in educational jargon and use words that are difficult for parents to understand. Most parents are not familiar with educational terms and all terms should be explained to parents in ways they can understand. Furthermore, acronyms should not be used; rather the name and purpose of the assessments and interventions should be stated and explained.

Typically, after the initial introductions are made, each individual responsible for conducting evaluations provides an oral report of their results. As a team, they tend to go around the table. At the end of the meeting, a determination is made whether the child qualifies for special education services. In other words, for parents, this brief meeting may change the educational history and outcomes for their child. Therefore, this can be a very emotional meeting.

IDEA defines special education as "specially designed instruction, at no cost to the parents, to meet the unique needs of the child with a disability" (300.39). "Specially designed instruction," defined as "adapting, as appropriate to the needs of the eligible child, the content, methodology, or delivery of instruction to meet the unique needs of the child that result from the child's disability." To be eligible for special education services, a student must have a disability and require specially designed instruction.

IDEA stresses using repeated evaluations to inform instruction and also to make changes to instruction based on these assessments. Furthermore, the law clearly states that the parents should be aware of their child's progress so they can support learning at home. Also, parents should be informed when teachers are concerned about their child's progress and made aware of what strategies are being used to improve and monitor their child's progress. In other words, the parents should be kept informed by the school.

In summary, to be eligible for special education and related services, a student must have a disability, the disability must adversely affect academic performance, and the student must require special education or related services. In other words, having a disability does not automatically qualify a student to receive services under IDEA. Thirteen disability categories are outlined in IDEA including:

1. Autism
2. Deaf-Blindness
3. Developmental Delayed (ages three to five)
4. Hearing Impairment (including deafness)
5. Emotional Disturbance
6. Mental Retardation
7. Multiple Disabilities
8. Orthopedic Impairment
9. Other Health Impairment
10. Specific Learning Disability
11. Speech or Language Impairment
12. Traumatic Brain Injury
13. Visual Impairment (including blindness)

CASE 3: WHAT SHOULD THE TEAM DECIDE?

Mrs. White is concerned that Nicholas is not reading fluently. Reading comprehension is another concern, as is his writing—especially grammar and spelling. Overall, Nicholas's performance is inconsistent in the classroom. Mrs. White is also concerned about Nicholas's behavior. Typically, he is a kind and caring student, but at times he lashes out at other students. As a result, Nicholas does not have many friends. In fact, several students have expressed that they do not want to work with Nicholas.

Mrs. White has reviewed Nicholas's file and knows that he lives with his mom who works full time and attends classes at night at the local community college. His mother is struggling to pay the bills and to find time to study and take care of her son. Sometimes Nicholas comes to school without doing his homework. At other times he states that his grandparents or his babysitter attempted to help him, but they did not know how to help him. He often looks tired and Mrs. White has gathered that he spends his evenings with a variety of people while his mother is in class.

It is January of Nicholas's third grade year and he has not made much progress since the beginning of the year. When he encounters a word he is not familiar with, he guesses based on the first letter or initial sound. Mrs. White has prompted him to sound out words, but he lacks decoding skills. Mrs. White has worked with Nicholas on phonemic awareness and phonics, but he just does not hear the sounds. Mrs. White mentioned this to his mother at the first parent-teacher conference and she stated that she is not a phonetic reader and could not decode either. Nicholas's mother also shared that there was a history of learning disabilities in the family and most of the males had struggled in school.

At this point Mrs. White had met with Nicholas's mother three times to discuss his lack of progress in reading and writing. She shared samples of his writing with the frequent misspellings. His mother was also aware of his poor grades on his weekly spelling tests. She stated that they studied the words each night, but when it came time to take the test, he would miss most of the words. She wondered if he had test anxiety.

His mother also shared that she reads to him as many nights as she can. After the first meeting, she had begun asking him questions as she reads and noticed that he was not able to recall simple things like the names of characters, important events, nor other main ideas. She added that he seemed to like to be read to and liked the time that they spent together sitting in his bed reading; however, she was concerned. His mother also stated that he does not read on his own and shows no interest in books other than when they are being read to him.

Mrs. White knew that state assessments were approaching and Nicholas's mother was also concerned. Being a new teacher, Mrs. White asked the principal for the paperwork and filled it out to refer Nicholas for special education services. She knew his mother was in agreement so there was no concern that this meeting would go smoothly. Mrs. White had tried her best, but she felt that Nicholas needed specialized assistance in a small group setting outside the classroom. The paperwork went home and was returned the following day; further indication that his mother was concerned.

The Student Support Team meeting was scheduled next week and Mrs. White gathered her grade book with Nicholas's failing spelling grades, the results of his reading comprehension tests, and also the fluency measures from the beginning and middle of the year. She also jotted down several notes about times in the class when Nicholas had verbally lashed out at other students. She felt prepared for the meeting and knew that Nicholas's mother was eager for him to get the help that he needed. After all, Mrs. White had done everything that she could, but she had twenty-seven other students in the classroom and she had to meet their needs as well.

Mrs. White went to the conference room for the scheduled meeting. When she arrived there was a special education teacher whom she knew, but had not really had a chance to interact with. The principal was also at the meeting. Mr. Barry introduced himself as the school psychologist and the guidance counselor, Mr. Thompson, was there as well. They were all chatting and talking when Nicholas's mother arrived.

Nicholas's mother entered the room and was immediately alarmed by how many people were there—people that she did not know. She had taken the day off from work to attend the meeting and to catch up on some homework so she wore old jeans and a t-shirt. After all, she knew most everyone in the school and she did not expect all of these people to be at the meeting—people that she had not met before. She thought the meeting was another parent-teacher conference.

The principal, Mr. Robertson, began the meeting by asking everyone to introduce themselves and state their position. Next, he asked Mrs. White to describe why she had called the meeting. Mrs. White shared with the team that Nicholas entered third grade reading below grade level and continues to read below grade level. She also stated that he failed most of his reading and spelling tests and his writing was also poor. Finally, Mrs. White stated that Nicholas had become angry on several occasions and had verbally and physically lashed out at other students.

Mrs. White also shared that she had several meetings with Nicholas's mom this year and his mother had shared that her brother, Nicholas's uncle, had a learning disability and her father, Nicholas's grandfather, probably did as well, but it was never diagnosed. Mrs. White also described her behavioral concerns noting that other students were becoming fearful of him. She ended by stating that she had done everything that she could for Nicholas, but it was not enough and she had to consider the needs of the other students in her class. She felt strongly that Nicholas needed extra help outside the classroom.

Questions to Ponder

1. In your opinion, had Mrs. White done everything necessary? Why or why not?
2. Was Mrs. White prepared for the meeting? What could she have done differently to prepare for the meeting? List the materials that would have been helpful at the meeting.
3. Was Nicholas's mother prepared for the meeting? Whose job is it to prepare her for the meeting?
4. Mrs. White stated that she had twenty-seven other students in her class. State some ways that teachers can meet the needs of students struggling academically or behaviorally while also meeting the needs of all other students. What are some strategies and interventions that would be appropriate?
5. What accommodations and interventions would you recommend be included in the Intervention Plan? Why? Make sure you address all areas of concern.
6. Was new information shared with Nicholas's mother at the meeting? If so, was this the appropriate way to share that information?

Activities to Complete

1. Conduct a Child Study meeting. Assign roles: principal, guidance counselor, school psychologist, Mrs. White, special education teacher, Nicholas's mom.

2. Create an intervention plan for Nicholas. What interventions or accommodations should be implemented? How long should the plan be implemented prior to the team reconvening?
3. Based on the weaknesses outlined (spelling, reading comprehension, reading decoding, and writing) determine Evidence-Based Practices appropriate for a third grader. Possible sites to visit include http://ies.ed.gov/ncee/wwc/ and http://www.bestevidence.org/.

CASE 4: WHAT ARE THE NEXT STEPS?

Chris Martin is an eighth grader at Madison Middle School in San Francisco, California. He moved to California three years ago from Atlanta, Georgia. Chris is the oldest of four boys in his family. His mother, Fey, moved the family to California to take a new job. This position required her to leave family and friends behind back East and move to an area where she knows no one. It has been a difficult transition for her and the boys.

Fey enjoys her new job and living in California. When she moved with the boys, her husband remained in Georgia. They are now divorced and she has recently started dating. She has dated several men, but the boys don't seem to like any of them. Now that the boys are older—fourteen, twelve, ten, and nine—and can take care of themselves, she feels that it is her time to have some fun and meet new people. She works hard and supports all four boys with little financial help from her ex-husband. She deserves to have fun.

Chris is a smart boy and his teachers have always commented that if he applied himself then his grades would improve. He was previously tested for special education services, but was not found eligible. In fact, his reading and writing abilities were above average and his math was in the average range. Additionally, scores on the intelligence tests, completed in third grade, were in the above average range. Despite this, Chris's grades are mainly Cs with the occasional B and D.

Chris wants to be an artist and says that he does not need to graduate high school to achieve that goal. He is the oldest and is having an especially difficult time adjusting to his parents' divorce. He and his brothers want the family back together again and Chris wants to move back to Georgia. His entire family lives in Georgia and he has friends there. He is also upset with his mother for leaving his father and hates that she is dating. It seems that his mother has really changed since the move and she isn't at home much anymore. She is very busy with her social life.

Chris is currently taking an advanced art class. His teacher, Ms. Temple, had originally thought very highly of Chris's talents. However, it has come to Ms. Temple's attention that Chris has been drawing disturbing pictures during class. Most of these drawings are violent. Chris has been drawing pictures of a woman that appears to be his mother with stab wounds or her head chopped off. The pictures are detailed and Ms. Temple must admit that they are well done, but she is concerned about the content of the pictures.

She asks Chris to stay after class and after all the other students leave, she asks Chris about the drawings. Chris becomes very upset and states that he is doing his work in her class, has completed all the assignments, and these are "just pictures." Ms. Temple asks Chris who the subject is in the pictures and he does not respond. She asks Chris if he is upset about anything and he leaves the room abruptly.

The next day, Chris enters class right before the bell rings and takes his regular seat. He seems to be avoiding eye contact with Ms. Temple. She introduces the lesson for the day and calls on Chris when she poses a question to the class, but he does not respond. In fact, he is staring blankly straight ahead and does not seem to notice that Ms. Temple and the rest of the class are starring at him. "Chris," "Chris," Ms. Temple says loudly. He rustles and asks, "What?" as he looks around the room and notices that all eyes are on him. Ms. Temple asks another student the same question, but this incident adds to her recent concerns.

Before the dismissal bell rings, Chris gathers his materials and is ready to dart out the door. Ms. Temple wonders if he is trying to avoid her or if he is trying to assure that he will not be detained after class. She dismisses the class as usual. After class ends, she notices that there is a piece of paper sticking out of the desk where Chris typically sits and she retrieves it. When she pulls the paper out of the desk, to her horror it is a picture of her with her head in a noose hanging from a tree. It is very graphic and detailed. She immediately heads to the principal's office. This student is a danger and she cannot have him return to her class.

Questions to Ponder

1. What do you think the principal's response will be? Is it appropriate to remove Chris from Ms. Temple's class? Why or why not?
2. Should Chris be punished? If so, what should his punishment be?
3. Should Chris be considered a student who possibly has a disability? Why or why not?
4. Should Chris be referred for special education services? If so, what disability category?
5. If you were Chris's teacher, would you have done things differently?
6. If you were Ms. Temple would you notify others inside or outside the school? If so, who?

Activities to Complete

1. Search state and national statistics for the number of students that are suspended annually.
2. Develop a behavior plan for Chris including measurable goals.
3. Hold a meeting with the principal to discuss your concerns.
4. Develop a plan for Ms. Temple to implement when Chris returns to her room.

THREE

Individualized Education Program

The Individualized Education Program (IEP) is a written document, developed by a school-based multidisciplinary team and the parents outlining the student's educational and related services. The IEP contains sections including the child's current academic, behavioral, and functional performance; special education services and related services; participation with nondisabled peers; and participation in state and district assessments.

The IEP is based on the unique needs of the student. IEPs are developed and implemented for one year and also contain sections outlining the child's strengths and weaknesses, goals, accommodations, academic progress, and most recent eligibility information. The IEP addresses what services will be provided, the location of the services, dates services will begin and end, and how often they will be provided.

The IEP goals must be specific and measurable and include a statement outlining how the goals will be measured. Parents must receive reports outlining progress toward annual goals throughout the year. Goals are based on the student's present level of performance and may address areas such as social skills, academics, behavior, or self-help. IEP goals should provide educational benefit to the student and should be attainable. Beginning at the age of sixteen, the IEP must address transition. Transition services are designed to prepare the student for leaving the school setting and what services and supports will be provided.

Classroom and testing accommodations are also included in the IEP. Classroom accommodations include things such as sitting the student in an area of least distractions within the classroom, additional time to complete tests and assignments, and reading of test and other instructional materials. Testing accommodations may include things such as reading of test items, alternative means of assessment, and specific recommendations for the format of the test. General education teachers as well as special education teachers are responsible for implementing accommodations in the classroom and when tests are administered. Accommodations may also include personnel such as an instructional assistant or nursing service.

The need for related services is determined at eligibility meetings. The IEP specifically outlines how often the services will be provided, who will provide these services, and in what setting. The location and frequency of these services may change with each IEP meeting. Related services include services such as physical therapy, occupational therapy, adaptive physical education, speech and language services, transportation, school health services, and counseling. Again, these services are based on the student's unique needs.

IDEA requires that a child be provided with a free appropriate public education (FAPE) in the least restrictive environment (LRE). Therefore, the location of services and the extent to which students will be educated with nondisabled peers must be discussed at each IEP meeting and included in each IEP.

Additionally, the IEP team must also consider the following factors outlined in IDEA:

- If the child's behavior impedes his own learning or the learning of others
- The language needs of the child if he has limited English proficiency
- The communication needs of the child
- If the child is blind or visually impaired
- If the child is deaf or hard of hearing
- The need for assistive technology devices or services

Parents are a key member of the IEP team, but often feel intimidated by the process and especially the meeting. Teachers and other school personnel frequently use educational terms unfamiliar to the parents. These meetings are also typically rushed and the parents sometimes don't know what questions to ask. Parents must grant permission for the IEP to be implemented. If parents have limited English proficiency, are deaf, or are blind, an interpreter or translator should be provided during the meeting. The school must arrange for these services. Furthermore, parental rights and other communication with the parents, such as arranging meetings, should be provided in the parents' native language.

Parents are granted due process rights through the IEP and if the parents are in disagreement with the IEP, they may exercise their due process rights. The IDEA encourages mediation as a first step to solve disagreements between a local educational agency and the parents. During mediation, the parents and a member of the school division meet with an impartial third party to attempt to solve disagreements. If a decision cannot be met through mediation, or if the parents decide not to attempt mediation, a due process hearing is the next step.

Due process hearings are like typical trials in which evidence is presented and witnesses testify. If one party does not agree with the outcome of the court hearing, they may file an appeal.

Websites

This document outlines the six major provisions of IDEA: http://wps. ablongman.com/wps/media/objects/1371/1404729/handouts/ Chapter02.pdf.

An overview of the IEP process is included here: http://www. parentcenterhub.org/repository/iep-overview/.

The United States Department of Education's Guide to the IEP process: http://www2.ed.gov/parents/needs/speced/iepguide/index. html.

Legal Issues and the IEP: http://www.wrightslaw.com/info/iep. index.htm.

CASE 5: IS THE SCHOOL PROVIDING APPROPRIATE SERVICES?

Rosemary is a kindergartner at Columbia Elementary School. She is a student with autism and began receiving special education services when she was two years old. In the first IEP developed, Rosemary's parents brought her to the local school three days per week and she received services from the speech pathologist, occupational therapist, and also educational services.

Rosemary's parents thought that she should receive more services, but the school stated that she was only two years old, had a short attention span, and was not able to attend for longer than an hour per day. Rosemary's parents also requested that she receive services five days per week rather than three days per week, but the school denied this request.

During the next IEP meeting, which was developed to provide services when Rosemary was three, Rosemary's parents again requested more services and for longer periods; however, the IEP again outlined services three days a week for one hour each day. The parents were required to bring her to school to receive these services. Rosemary's mother, Mrs. Marquette, had recently begun working and this created a hardship on her family. Mrs. Marquette reluctantly asked her new boss to change her schedule so she could come to work two hours later on Mondays, Wednesdays, and Fridays when Rosemary had services.

Mrs. Marquette's boss reluctantly agreed, but informed her that he was unsure how long he could allow her to do this. After all, the company was only open during normal business hours, from 8 a.m. to 5 p.m.

each day and during the time of Mrs. Marquette's absence, he would need to find someone to sit at the receptionist desk. Mrs. Marquette hated asking her boss to make these changes and worried that she may lose her job based on this request.

When Rosemary turned four, a new IEP was developed. Mrs. Marquette had done a lot of research on the internet and had learned about Applied Behavior Analysis (ABA). She wanted Rosemary to have ABA services and knew from her research that only someone trained in ABA could provide these services.

Since Rosemary had begun daycare when Mrs. Marquette returned to work, her teachers were constantly commenting about her lack of social skills, stated that she did not interact with other students, and also that she had tantrums throughout the day. The manager at the daycare center had spoken to Mr. and Mrs. Marquette and informed them that if the tantrums increased in intensity and frequency then Rosemary's parents may need to find another daycare center.

The manager further explained that when Rosemary had a tantrum, it required multiple staff members to attend to her. After each tantrum, it took Rosemary a while to calm down and this also required a staff member to sit with her until she was ready to return to the group activities. Finally, the daycare manager explained that they may not be equipped to deal with Rosemary and her unique needs. Mrs. Marquette had to work to support the family and she worried that Rosemary would be kicked out of daycare.

At this IEP meeting, the team assembled and presented Mr. and Mrs. Marquette with the newly developed IEP. This IEP outlined that Rosemary would receive two hours of services three days per week. On Mondays, she would receive thirty minutes of occupational therapy and then be in a classroom with other preschoolers for ninety minutes. On Wednesdays, Rosemary would receive speech services for thirty minutes and then would attend the preschool class for ninety minutes, and on Fridays, Rosemary would be in the preschool class for the entire two hours.

Mr. and Mrs. Marquette were glad that the school offered another hour of services three days per week, but Mrs. Marquette worried about her job. How could she ask her boss for additional time off? He would certainly fire her. After all, other employees were already complaining about her coming in late three days per week and were stating that they could not get their work done.

The Marquettes requested that the school provide transportation for Rosemary. They could come to the house and pick her up in the morning, take her to school, and then drop her off at daycare. The school refused. They stated that the bus seats are too large for preschoolers and they also pointed out that the daycare center was outside the school boundaries.

Mr. and Mrs. Marquette also described the behaviors that were occurring at the daycare center and asked for IEP goals to specifically address her lack of social skills. The school stated that Rosemary interacted with other peers in the school setting and therefore refused to add a goal for social skills. The Marquettes also brought up Rosemary's tantrums. Again, the school stated that they had not seen any tantrums.

Finally, the preschool teacher suggested that the Marquettes provide the daycare center with additional information about students with autism. The daycare center had stated that Rosemary always had a tantrum when there was a change in schedule. The preschool teacher stated that this is common with students with autism and perhaps the daycare setting could assure that they follow the established schedule and the tantrums would be alleviated. Furthermore, that is what she did in the preschool room and it worked for Rosemary.

Lastly, the Marquettes requested ABA services for Rosemary. The school members discussed this and asked the Marquettes why they wanted these services. Mrs. Marquette had done a lot of research and confidently answered that she believed these services would help Rosemary with transitioning, behavior management, and also with work completion.

Rosemary's preschool teacher stated that she had never seen Rosemary have a tantrum. Furthermore, she prepared Rosemary for transitions by providing a schedule for the day and warnings prior to a transition and this was working fine. Finally, she showed the Marquettes Rosemary's notebook which outlined the number of trials she completed daily and her progress throughout the year. She stated that these procedures were based on ABA and therefore they were already providing Rosemary with those services.

The Marquettes reluctantly signed the IEP. They were not happy with the services and felt that Rosemary needed more services for longer periods. After all, she would be starting kindergarten next year and would be expected to be at school all day. They worried that two hours three days per week was not enough and that it would be too large of a transition to go to five full days the following year. Mrs. Marquette also did not know how or what to say to her boss. She knew that her schedule was already creating a hardship at work.

Questions to Ponder

1. Was the school providing appropriate services to Rosemary?
2. Were the services the Marquettes were requesting warranted?
3. In your opinion, does Rosemary require ABA services? Are the services the school is currently providing ABA services?
4. If you were Mr. and Mrs. Marquette, would you have signed the IEP?

5. If you were the Marquettes, what would you do next?
6. During the IEP meetings, school personnel repeatedly stated that they had not witnessed the behaviors described by Rosemary's parents. What are the legal requirements of the school? Do the behaviors need to occur in the school for services to be provided in the IEP?

Activities to Complete

1. Research ABA. What is ABA? In what ways do schools provide ABA services? Are there requirements for training school personnel on ABA services?
2. Assign roles and hold an IEP meeting.
3. Research services for students with autism. What are appropriate activities and interventions for social skills? What programs are appropriate for preschool students?
4. What are common difficulties that students with autism have in the school setting?
5. Create specific measurable goals to address Rosemary's behavioral and social difficulties described in this case. Develop materials to track progress toward these IEP goals.

CASE 6: WHAT SHOULD TOMMY DO NEXT YEAR?

Tommy is a senior at Lakeside High School. He has a specific learning disability and has been receiving special education services since he was in the second grade. In Tommy's current IEP, Tommy's services include self-contained English and collaborative courses for other core subjects (history, science, and math).

Tommy is also enrolled in the auto mechanics course offered at the vocational school and hopes to continue his education in this program, one additional year, when he graduates. He loves working on cars and is good at it, but his parents want him to go to a four-year college, just like they did. They feel that he should at least try college and his current IEP contains goals to prepare him for college.

Tommy recently turned eighteen and his parents are preparing for Tommy's last IEP meeting before he graduates. Tommy's parents plan to ask the school to update his testing so they can provide that information to the local college. They already contacted the college and they require testing that has been completed in the last two years to develop accommodations for Tommy.

Despite Tommy's efforts, he cannot convince his parents to let him finish his last year of the auto mechanics course. His plan is to attend the class daily and work part time. There is a comprehensive exam at the end of the course and he wants to finish the final year of the program. He worries that if he attends the local college he will have at least a one-year lapse in his coursework. He doesn't care about getting his hands dirty and that is what he wants to do for a living. As part of his IEP, he had to research his career of choice and he learned that auto mechanics made a lot of money.

While Tommy's parents are focused on college and what the college requires; Tommy is focused on finishing his auto mechanics schooling. He has an A average in the course. The reading is time consuming and he has to re-read materials and create notecards for himself to learn and remember all the vocabulary, but he is willing to do this because he enjoys the content. This is his most successful class and he is proud of his grade.

Tommy knows that remembering things is difficult for him and he really worries that if he has to stop the class and go to college then he will forget everything by the time he comes back to finish the course. He is convinced that he won't do well in college and will probably fail out during his first semester there; however, he may only enroll in the auto mechanics class in the fall. Therefore, if he goes to college, it will delay his enrollment in auto mechanics for at least one year. Why won't his parents listen?

Tommy's IEP meeting is scheduled during his resource class. He and his resource teacher, Mr. Simon, will go to the office together for the meeting. An instructional assistant will come in to cover Mr. Simon's class while he is at the meeting. Tommy does not know what to do. He wants to please his parents, but by pleasing them, he feels like he is giving up on his hopes and dreams and maybe even sabotaging them.

As Tommy and Mr. Simon walk to the office, Mr. Simon comments to Tommy that it looks like he has the weight of the world on his shoulders. Tommy quickly tells Mr. Simon that he and his parents have a difference of opinion about what he should do next year. Mr. Simon tells Tommy that since he is eighteen, he decides what goals he wants in his IEP. Furthermore, since he is eighteen, he is the one who will be signing his IEP; not his mother.

Questions to Ponder

1. Is it true that Tommy is the one that will sign his IEP since he is eighteen? Is this true in all states?
2. In your opinion, did the school prepare Tommy for his IEP meeting? Should Tommy have known earlier that he was the one signing the IEP since he turned eighteen?
3. Do you think Tommy's mother is aware that she is not signing the IEP? If not, should she have been informed in some way?
4. If you were Tommy, what would you do?

5. What are some things that the school could have done to prepare Tommy for the meeting? Be specific.

Activities to Complete

1. Write IEP goals to prepare Tommy for the auto mechanics course.
2. Write IEP goals to prepare Tommy to transition to college.
3. Research what schools typically do to prepare students for college.
4. Hold a mock IEP meeting. Who at the meeting will be responsible for telling Tommy's mother that Tommy is the one who signs the IEP? When during the meeting will his mother be told? What happens if she disagrees with this practice?

FOUR

Working with Parents

FAMILIES IN CRISIS

The discovery that a child has a disability can send a family into crisis mode. They may experience feelings such as surprise, confusion, anger, sorrow, denial, or fear. For some families, the attachment of a label to the worrying symptoms is a relief, but for others, it feels like a threat.

So many questions arise:

Is this my fault?
What does the label mean?
How does my vision of my child's future change?
Will my child be segregated at school?
Is the school making this up to hide its own failings?
How can the school fix my child?
What can I do to fix my child?

We cannot expect a parent who has just received this news, or who has lived with the knowledge of the disability for years, to act like parents of children without disabilities. They have been through an experience unlike those of other parents.

Think for a minute about what this process is like. Of course it varies from family to family and disability to disability. Some learn when the child is a newborn or infant that he has a genetic defect that results in various forms of disability. They may get support from the hospital and early infant special services programs.

Others have the belief that their child is developing like other children until he begins school. He is likely to experience failing report cards or repeated suspensions before the disability is identified. The identification may be a form of relief, since the confusing symptoms finally have a name. But since diagnosis does not result in a quick cure, the relief can be short lived.

FROM A PARENT'S VIEW

So now what?

We as parents have just lived through our child's eligibility meeting. That process was extremely difficult. In some ways, it seemed to be designed to be excruciating for the parents.

The way that the meeting was set up targeted us as outsiders from the beginning. We arrived about fifteen minutes early and were told to wait in the office. The meeting room was beyond the office, and as the other participants arrived they went back to the room. We knew a few of them, like our child's teacher, and they said hello but they did not stop to speak to us.

We could hear them back in the room chatting with each other as they arrived. Clearly, they knew each other. Then, when five people, mostly strangers to us, had gathered, they asked us to enter the room. Walking into that meeting with all eyes on us was terrifying. They smiled and introduced themselves, but of course we didn't remember a single name. If only we had been in the room as people gathered, we could get to know who they were as they arrived.

We continued to feel like outsiders as they talked about our child. The room full of "experts" threw around incomprehensible numbers, terms, and acronyms with only minimal explanations to us. The social worker had interviewed us at home a few weeks earlier and she read her report describing our family as if we weren't even there.

They gave us a copy of "Parental Rights in Special Education," a document that was long and totally confusing. There was no way we could read it at that meeting. It would take all our experience as college students to digest the legal information it contained.

When they did ask if we had any questions or comments, we had no idea what to ask. It didn't seem appropriate to request that they go through the whole thing again but this time in English. Stating that we had no questions certainly did not mean that we understood what was happening.

The acronyms they used seemed to apply to the different disabilities they were considering. Is our child ADD? ADHD? LD? ED? ID? ASD? Of course we had heard of some of those, and had read up on others as we tried to figure out why our child was failing, but there were some new ones in the mix that day. We did understand that the label they decided on would have an important effect on the services our child got, so we tried to understand. We really tried.

In the end, they told us that our child did qualify as having a disability. We weren't sure if it was good news or bad news. The fact that she does have something wrong with her is not good, but at least she will get some help now.

We understand that getting that help involves another big meeting. How can we be more prepared for that meeting? We were determined to get more information or to hire an advocate to support us so that we can know what will be happening to our child.

RESOURCES FOR PARENTS

You as the general education teacher may be the first person to suggest to the parents that their child has a disability. At this point you are their primary resource. The news that a referral to special education is being made most likely comes from you. Ideally, you have prepared them well for the news. The better their relationship with you, the easier the process will be for them.

You have begun the year with a positive phone call and have made it clear that you believe in their child. As the academic or behavioral concerns begin to mount, you send home work samples or behavior charts frequently. You ask them to give you information on their child's background, motivations, and strengths. You use that information to work with the child and keep the parents up to date on any progress. You work hard at developing your relationship into a strong partnership.

At the same time, you make sure that your own knowledge about the special education process is complete and accurate. While not suggesting any particular disability to the parents, you learn about characteristics of students with different disabilities as well as effective teaching methods. You talk with the special educators and guidance counselors in your school about the student and about what procedures will be involved if a referral is made.

You also find out about resources for parents, knowing that the family will want to be as prepared as possible before the eligibility meeting. You are surprised at the variety and usefulness of the websites. They include basic information, legal advice, and sites that offer support from other parents of children with disabilities. You hold on to these, preparing to make them available if the child does have a disability.

As the process continues, you are at the mother's side, making sure she is comfortable at the meetings, interpreting information that she does not understand, and ensuring that her information and opinions are heard. You have come to understand that you are her most important resource, and that your student is the beneficiary when his mother is informed and confident.

ADVOCACY

Some parents can be a pain. They seem to be angry all the time, and most of their communication comes in the form of demands. When it comes time for an eligibility or IEP meeting with that family, the district knows that they need to send someone from the special education office. Both parents will be there, and they will have their own ideas of what will help their child. They may challenge information that you as the teacher present, and threaten to file a due process procedure if they are not satisfied. You approach the meeting with trepidation. How can you prepare?

Most of your preparation should take place well before the meeting. The parents are much less likely to come into a meeting in fighting mode if they trust you and have seen evidence of their child's progress. They will trust you if you do three things:

1. Find a way to sincerely like their child, appreciating his strengths and understanding his needs.
2. Really listen to the parent, making an effort to see the child and situations from their point of view.
3. Communicate often.

Some students with disabilities are difficult to like. They may not relate well to you, or may refuse to comply with your directions. They may be sulky and unkind to other students. But you will need to find that seed of curiosity, special skill, or desire for affection that will enable you to develop a connection. Many students will not learn from you if they think that you don't like them, and parents will definitely feel the necessity to battle if they sense antagonism toward their child.

If parents come in angry about an event that took place at school, avoid the tendency to react defensively. Understand that the parent needs to vent and you should listen to what they have to say. You may not be able to fix the problem immediately—it may take consultation with other principals or the teacher, but if the parents feel that they have been heard, you have made an important step toward a solution.

Some items may be worked out through negotiation. For example, you might explain that a daily note is not possible but that you understand their need to know what is happening in the classroom. You propose a modified version of the accommodation, such as a weekly note for the first month and then a checklist completed by the student for the rest of the year. You both agree to work with the student on his ability to tell his parents about the day's events.

Another way to avoid contention at the IEP meeting is to keep the parents informed of their child's progress. Reports indicating progress toward meeting IEP goals are important, as are results of weekly Curriculum-Based Measurement (CBM) assessments. As described in the assessment chapter, these assessments are good indicators of academic success.

Graphic representations of CBM results at the IEP meeting assist everyone in understanding which goals have been met and which new ones need to be written.

However, the IEP meeting should not be the first time the parents have seen these graphs. If you are true partners, you are sharing them throughout the school year. Together you are working on ensuring that the progress line continues to rise. Remember that parents who make a fuss to ensure that their child gets a good education are doing their job. Every student needs an advocate, especially one who has a disability.

THE REALITY OF PARENTING A CHILD WITH A DISABILITY

As teachers we sometimes become impatient with parents of our students with disabilities. We think that they hover too much, get over-involved, and can be too demanding. Or we might think that they are too absent—they don't show up for IEP meetings or answer telephone calls.

At times we blame the parents, asserting that if only they would step back, the child would be more independent. If only they would come to school more often, the child would get better grades. A concept called "direction of effects" explains that sometimes our conclusions about cause and effect may in fact be turned the wrong way.

Perhaps the mother who is always checking to be sure her son has everything in his backpack or who comes to school to pick up forgotten books is doing this because she has experienced numerous negative effects from his lack of organization. We think that his organization would improve if she stopped shielding him from lower grades, but she knows that he will continue to forget and eventually fail. She has seen it happen.

Leo Kanner described the mothers of children who had autism as "refrigerator mothers" because they made little eye contact with their children and were not very physically close to them (Eisenberg, 1981). This blame directed at mothers was extremely hurtful and inaccurate until researchers began to reverse the description. It came to be seen that the lack of eye contact and physical closeness were innate characteristics of the children, and the parents' behavior was in response to their experiences in taking care of the child. Consider the following example.

Margaret was the teacher of students with profound disabilities in the middle school. She had been working hard on helping Jerome learn to feed himself and believed he was making progress. However, she knew that he would progress more quickly if his father would go through the feeding steps each morning at home. Margaret had demonstrated the process to the father, but each morning Jerome indicated that his father had fed his breakfast to him rather than letting him feed himself.

She complained of the father's noncompliance to her assistant principal, Albert, who asked her how long it takes her to get Jerome to feed himself each day. Margaret admitted that it took her close to two hours. He asked if Jerome's father had a job. In fact, he had two jobs and was barely making ends meet. As they talked, it became clear to Margaret that Jerome's father was doing all he could to take care of him. Just dressing him took close to one half hour each morning. There was no way he could spend two hours helping Jerome feed himself and still get to work on time.

Being the parent of a child with a disability is hard. It is scary, discouraging, and never ending. It is also lonely. If your son Paul has autism, he likely has few friends. He doesn't get invited on play dates or to birthday parties. At the park you spend your time making sure Paul doesn't get into dangerous situations so you don't have the chance to chat with other mothers as the children play together. You like to go out to restaurants, but it is a huge hassle to get Paul to sit and eat in a strange place. So you stay home. It's just easier.

Parenting a child with a disability is also tiring. Imagine how tired Jerome's father is at the end of the day after toileting and dressing him, getting him into his wheelchair, feeding him, getting him on the bus, working all day, and then repeating the procedure in reverse at the end of the day. He would love to have someone to help with Jerome's care, but he can't afford it.

Or consider Mrs. Robinson whose daughter Alicia has attention deficit/hyperactivity disorder (ADHD). Getting through the homework process each day is a nightmare. She has set up designated homework stations for each of her daughters, but while Frances will sit and complete her work, Alicia is another story. She is continually jumping up, playing, and talking instead of concentrating. Mrs. Robinson knows she shouldn't, but she gets frustrated and yells at Alicia. The work still doesn't get done, and they both go to bed upset and exhausted.

What about the parents who never show up? They don't respond to any attempts to schedule meetings by mail, phone, or email. They don't come to school events. It seems that they don't care. Jerome's father used to come to the IEP meetings. But now that his son is in eighth grade, he feels like his efforts have not really paid off. The school is going to do what they want to do regardless of his suggestions. So he just lets them write the IEPs without him. He signs them and sends them back.

Review the scenario described in "From a Parent's View" at the beginning of this chapter. Imagine that the parents in that description had in fact been a single mother who herself had never graduated from high school. School was never a good place for her. She was bullied, unsure, scared, and felt like a failure when she was there. Going to meetings at the school makes her feel the same way. When the school contacts her she sometimes has trouble reading the letters. When teachers call, it is usually bad news like it was when she was a kid. It is better not to answer.

It will take a determined effort on the part of some teacher or administrator to make this mother feel trusting enough to attend an IEP meeting,
and to ensure that she feels truly included and valued when she is there.

A VALUABLE RESOURCE

Finding ways to help parents of children with disabilities become truly
involved in their child's education, and to ease their burden, is worth-
while. It may take effort to establish a true partnership, but both partners,
and the child, benefit. You as a teacher learn more about the capabilities
of your student and gain insight into the life they lead. The parent gains
organization and teaching skills that you impart and develops confidence
that she is not alone. You are in this together.

Additional Resources

> This site gives a clear picture of Asperger syndrome: http://www.
> ninds.nih.gov/disorders/asperger/detail_asperger.htm.
> Pacer's National Parent Center on Transition and Employment: http://
> www.pacer.org/transition/.
> Possibilities: A Financial Resources for Parents of Children with Dis-
> abilities: http://www.pacer.org/publications/possibilities/.
> Center for Parent Information and Resources: http://www.
> parentcenterhub.org/.
> A Parent Guide to Special Education, the IEP Process, and School
> Success: http://www.understandingspecialeducation.com/.

CASE 7: WHAT CAN PARENTS DO?

Carla and Bob were happy to be moving to their new house in the country with their two children. They loved living near the beautiful moun-
tains and looked forward to family outings. Beth would be starting kindergarten at the little elementary school a short drive away. Matthew
would be in fourth grade.

Beth would have no problems. She was sharp, outgoing, and had a
happy disposition. Carla knew that she would adjust to school and new
friends easily. But Matthew was a different story. When he was in third
grade, after two years of many issues in school, he was identified as
having Asperger syndrome.

Carla knew that Matthew was somewhat different when he was about
three years old. He was very verbal and talked animatedly with adults,
but had difficulties relating to other children. He loved books and was
reading well by the time he was four. When he went to playmates' homes
he tended to sit and read their books instead of interacting with them.

In kindergarten it became clear that work completion would be a significant problem. Matthew wanted to spend time in the reading corner. His handwriting and math skills were much weaker than his verbal abilities, but he resisted doing any work in those areas. He was not oppositional or difficult—he would just drift away from the tasks, finding pleasure in his own company. Very little work got done.

The pattern continued in first and second grades. It was so frustrating to Carla. Matthew's teachers complained that he was lazy, that he didn't care, that he couldn't pay attention. His mother saw his delight in learning, his curiosity, his pleasure in word play, and his clear intelligence. Why couldn't he do well in school? He would come home frustrated and angry. He wanted to do well, to please his mother and his teachers, but staying on task and working on areas that were weak seemed to be beyond his capabilities.

To make things worse, he really didn't have any friends. He never talked about inviting boys to play at his house, and he never received invitations. When Carla joined his class for field trips, she saw that several of the other boys teased him when they weren't avoiding him. They called him names and dared him to engage in forbidden activities. Once he got in trouble for leaving the playground to find a treasure that the boys assured him was hidden close by.

School was a misery for Carla's smart, verbal boy. At times she thought that the only way for him to learn in peace would be to teach him at home. Then in third grade his teacher proposed having him tested and it was determined that his characteristics met those of a child with Asperger syndrome. They wrote an IEP for him and things changed.

Matthew did not need a great deal of individual teaching, but he did need accommodations. His IEP specified that he would have an individual calendar to help him stay organized, a daily checklist with consequences for missing and completed work, shortened math worksheets, and weekly communications with Carla. He also received practice in pragmatic skills (social interactions) from the speech and language pathologist.

His third grade teacher and the speech therapist implemented these goals faithfully and Matthew had a much better year. His grades rose, teachers were no longer frustrated with him, and he began to feel less like a failure. Carla and Bob understood that the IEP would also be in effect in his new school in fourth grade and they looked forward to continued success for Matthew. But that did not happen.

Carla took a copy of the IEP to the school in July when she registered the children. The secretary said that she would pass it on to the teacher. In addition, Carla spoke to Matthew's teacher, Mrs. Winter, at the open house who, while she was busy that night, said that she had seen the IEP. But, after two weeks of school, Matthew had the haunted, confused look he had worn in second grade. He said that he didn't like his new school.

The teacher yelled at him, the work was too hard, and the other kids didn't like him.

Three weeks after that, Mrs. Winter asked Carla and Bob to come in for a meeting. They kept the afternoon appointment with trepidation. They had been in similar meetings before Matthew was identified as needing special education.

Mrs. Winter opened the meeting. "Matthew is obviously bright, but it looks like he can't be bothered with completing his assignments. Most of his daily work is shoved into his desk unfinished and he spends his time reading a book he brings to school. When I encourage him to get to work, he will start on it, but before I know it he has his nose in the book again. Also, he has not tried to get to know his new classmates. It sometimes looks like he is avoiding them."

When Carla brought up the IEP, Mrs. Winter nodded. "I read that, but I don't think it will work here. It is not fair to the other students to give him shorter assignments, and those checklists won't work. We only have a speech teacher one day a week, and her schedule is already full. Matthew will just have to start buckling down and getting things done. Otherwise he is in danger of failing fourth grade."

Carla and Bob were stunned. What could they do? They knew that the goals and accommodations on the IEP did help Matthew be successful in school, but it looked like they would not follow them here. Would they have to move back to their previous home? What other recourse did they have?

Questions to Ponder

1. What should be Carla and Bob's next move? List the steps they should take to ensure that Matthew's IEP is being implemented appropriately.
2. Assume that some of their first options, such as meeting with the principal, are not successful. Detail what else they could do.
3. Describe Mrs. Winter. What is her classroom like? How might it be organized? What could she do to make it a place where students like Matthew are more successful?
4. Develop a sample of the daily checklist with consequences for missing and completed work that was implemented in third grade. Be specific, including the exact consequences that might work for Matthew.
5. List the goals that are likely to be on the IEP that was initially developed. Include the pragmatic skills goals that the speech therapist was addressing.

Activities to Complete

1. Rewrite the case from Mrs. Winter's point of view.
2. Rewrite the case from Matthew's third grade teacher's point of view.
3. Research Asperger syndrome. Develop a list of characteristics and educational needs for student who have this syndrome. How do Matthew's characteristics fit the descriptions you have found?
4. Look at the film illustrating the plight of parents of children with autism: Refrigerator Mothers http://www.snagfilms.com/films/title/refrigerator_mothers.

   a. What did you learn about the experiences of parents of people with disabilities?
   b. The "children" in the film are now adults. What does that tell you about the responsibility that parents have for their children with autism?
   c. What does the film say about the importance of parents as advocates?
   d. At the end a parent describes a good partnership with doctors, noting that the doctors value the fact that parents do know the most about the child. How can teachers make use of this?

CASE 8: WHO IS RESPONSIBLE?

This case is told from two points of view: Susan Dickey, high school social studies teacher, and Mary Williams, mother of Angela, a high school student.

Susan Dickey

I have been teaching social studies at Mountain High School for ten years and I love it. I love my subject and I love getting students excited about history. I try to use methods that get the student actively involved every day, keeping their minds and even their bodies engaged. Over the years I have found techniques that work well, and my classroom is a happy, busy place.

One of the reasons for this success is my close working relationship with Helen Grange, our special education teacher. She co-teaches with me for two periods and I have gained a lot of respect for her. Her focus on providing the necessary supports for all students has helped me to plan lessons that ensure that every student learns the important historical concepts.

The Universal Design for Learning (UDL) principles have provided a very useful framework for our planning sessions. We have even included some of her students with intellectual disabilities in my class. They are able to learn the major ideas that we present, even if they express their ideas and knowledge in ways that are different from the other students.

Helen and I often talk about the fact that families are so much less involved at the high school level than they are in the lower grades. Perhaps about half of our parents come to the annual open house, and that is usually the last time we see them. Few parents sign up for parent conferences. We keep looking for ways to attract parents to academic activities at this level.

Mary Williams

My daughter Angela is a good girl. She was a happy toddler, my first child. It didn't bother her that she walked late and took a long time to learn to talk in sentences. I thought that she would catch up when she got into school, but that did not happen. They called me after Christmas in her kindergarten year and said that they wanted to evaluate her. I didn't know what it was all about, but I told them to go ahead.

Then came the first of many meetings that were scary and frustrating for me. Most of the time I did not know what was going on. My only choice, really, was to agree with them if I wanted Angela to get a good education. They told me at the first meeting that she had an intellectual disability, or mental retardation, as they called it then. I was surprised—I thought that she was just a little slow to develop. Since I have had two more girls I can see the difference, but I couldn't understand it then. It was all a confusing mystery to me.

Every year after that I would come into a room full of unfamiliar people and they would talk about her progress and new goals. But I never felt that they wanted my opinion or any information from me. They already had their minds made up. So I signed the paper like they asked.

Angela was happy in school, and she was learning even though she was slow. By fourth grade she could read pretty well and she learned to do addition and subtraction. She could even write a little bit. She was not at all like my other daughters, but she was doing okay. After that year, though, I stopped going to IEP meetings and they sent the papers home for me to sign. It seemed like such a waste of time, and it was hard for me to miss work. They were doing fine without me.

I have never gotten to know any of Angela's teachers very well. For a while she had new teachers every year, and we did not communicate often. After I stopped going to those useless IEP meetings I lost touch with them. I was surprised when I started getting more information from her teacher once Angela started high school. Ms. Grange is different.

She started by calling me at the beginning of Angela's freshman year. She said that she would be her case manager for the four years Angela was at the school. And she asked me my opinion on how Angela learns! No teacher ever asked me anything like that before. They were always telling me things. I felt like this was going to be different.

Susan Dickey

I have learned so much from Ms. Grange. She is constantly looking to for ways to draw parents into the process of planning for their children. It seems like she has hit on some effective solutions to the problem. She contacts parents frequently, and she never gives up. I can see that she really values what parents have to say about their children—she truly believes that they know their child best, and that she can learn from them. I am going to try some of her techniques with the other students in my classes.

A good example of how she has made it work is in the area of transition planning. After she gains the trust of most of her parents through her relentless reaching out to them, she helps them to understand how important they are in planning for their child's future. While in general education we talk about going to college or working after graduation; in special education it is a different story.

Without the support of school, life after graduation can be very difficult for students with disabilities unless careful plans are made. I have been involved with this process for Angela Williams and I find it fascinating. Since Angela's mother will be her "case manager" after Angela graduates, she needs to be fully involved in the process as well. Ms. Grange convinced Mrs. Williams that she was an integral part of Angela's transition team and has sought her opinion at every step along the way.

Together we have helped Angela become more of an advocate for herself, have identified Angela's and her mother's goals for her, and connected with agencies that can give her employment and possibly housing after she leaves school. The process is not yet complete, but before Angela graduates, she will have some good life skills, will know how to ask for what she needs, and will have all the information necessary to access community resources.

One more example of Ms. Grange's good understanding of parent experiences and situations is the video that she gives every student. The video is a reminder of the steps to a good transition and gives information on how to contact the relevant community agencies. She knows that students and parents are often overwhelmed by information we give them, and that being able to see it on a video after school supports are ended can be extremely useful.

Ms. Grange has taught me so many things. Her focus on expending effort in reaching and educating families may be one of the most valuable. If we are going to give our students an education that lasts, we need to draw in families in every way we can.

Questions to Ponder

1. What would a plan for reaching high school parents look like? Make a list of the steps you could take to ensure that parents of students with disabilities become more involved in their education.
2. What types of supports do you think that Angela will need after she graduates? Will she be able to work or live on her own?
3. What could Angela's elementary and middle school teachers have done to keep Mrs. Williams involved?
4. How do you think that Ms. Dickey can use the techniques of parent involvement with her general education students?
5. How do you think that Ms. Dickey can us the techniques of transition planning with her general education students?

Activities to Complete

1. Learn more about transition planning from the IRIS module athttp://iris.peabody.vanderbilt.edu/module/tran/. Respond to Paula Kholer's talk on the IRIS module on page 7 when she talks about involving parents. What does she mean when she says that "we limit them [families] based on our perception of what they should be doing"? What can we do to avoid this?
2. Look at the transition pages that are part of your school's IEP form. What do you notice? What part do you think would be the most challenging?
3. Write a sample transition plan for Angela.
4. Write a case describing the ideal teachers (general and special education) from a parent's point of view.

FIVE
Co-Teaching

Co-teaching, or having two teachers in a classroom, is an increasingly popular method of providing special education services in the least restrictive environment. The two teachers, most likely a general educator and a special educator, have different educational preparation and backgrounds. Related service providers (such as speech language pathologist, occupational therapist, and physical therapist) may also partner with a general or special education teacher. Each teacher may have different resources and approaches that may complement each other and enhance the learning for all students in the classroom.

Both teachers are jointly responsible for planning and implementing instruction. At first, the planning requires a great deal of time, but requires less time as the teachers become more familiar with each other and the varying modes of instruction. Some administrators assure that teachers have similar planning blocks when they are co-teaching. Issues surrounding grading, behavior management, classroom management, routines and procedures, and teachers' pet peeves need to be discussed up front. It is important that both teachers present a united approach in front of the students at all times.

Marilyn Friend (2008) outlined six models of instruction for co-teaching. The models are one teach, one observe; one teach, one assist; station teaching; parallel teaching; alternative teaching; and team teaching. The models will be explained next.

ONE TEACH, ONE OBSERVE

This model, designed to be used infrequently, allows one teacher to teach the entire class while the other teacher observes. Often students' Individualized Education Programs (IEPs) require behavioral observations and it is not possible to teach a lesson and observe simultaneously. One of the advantages of two teachers in the classroom is that one can observe. During planning, the co-teachers decide which one of them will observe. Observations may be for one student, a group of students, or the entire class. The goals of the observation are established, the materials for documenting observations, and the length are established beforehand. After observations, both teachers should analyze the observation data.

ONE TEACH, ONE ASSIST

This model tends to be overused and should only occasionally be used in the classroom. When implementing this model, one teacher is responsible for delivering instruction while the other teacher circulates the room and provides assistance to students, as needed.

STATION TEACHING

Utilizing a station teaching approach, the teachers teach different materials to students in different areas of the room. Students rotate to stations throughout the room. The stations typically include working with each of the teachers and also activities that can be completed independently. This arrangement allows for smaller groups of students and two teachers assisting with instruction, classroom transitions, and classroom management.

PARALLEL TEACHING

Parallel teaching is when the content is divided between the two teachers and they are both teaching the same materials simultaneously. Using this method of instruction, students may be divided and taught the same material utilizing the same or different instructional approaches. The advantage to this method is that the student-to-teacher ratio is cut in half allowing for more student-teacher interaction and teachers may supervise the class more effectively. The disadvantage is that the noise level in the classroom may increase or when using different methods, students may want to be in the group other than the one they are assigned.

ALTERNATIVE TEACHING

Alternative teaching is often used when a group of students were absent or need remediation. One teacher takes responsibility for the larger group of students while the other works with a purposeful group of students. It is important when utilizing this method that teachers alternate between the small group and large group so one teacher is not always teaching one particular group. By rotating roles, this sends a message to students that both teachers are capable of teaching the class. Also, it is important to remember that the smaller groups are formed purposefully and they should not consist of the same students all the time.

TEAM TEACHING

Team teaching requires the most amount of planning and it also requires that both teachers have knowledge of the content. Using this approach, both teachers deliver instruction throughout a lesson. This approach is highly integrated and requires a great deal of planning. This is a planned event and not one teacher showing up and interjecting comments during the lesson.

In Summary, although co-teaching has been used for a number of years, there is still confusion about what actually occurs during a co-taught lesson. Also, teaching is typically done in isolation and sometimes teachers take advantage of having another teacher in the classroom. Some teachers also feel anxious about having another teacher in their classroom observing and possibly judging what occurs in the room. Therefore, it is important for co-teaching teams to also talk about what co-teaching is and what it is not.

Co-teaching is not one teacher teaching while the other makes phone calls, makes copies, grades papers, or completes other instructional duties. Also, it is not one teacher planning the lesson and the other showing up and walking around the classroom assisting students academically and behaviorally. It is also not trading off subjects to teach so one teaches one lesson and the other teacher teaches another subject. Rather, it is a shared responsibility in the classroom for teaching all the students.

Co-teaching has many advantages for the students and the teachers. Students in co-taught classes learn more and achieve higher. General and special educators are prepared and trained differently and each brings unique skills to the classroom. Furthermore, they may have different resources and materials that can be shared. Teachers can learn instructional methods, management styles, and organizational strategies from each other.

Websites

A video of co-teaching in action: https://www.youtube.com/watch?v= ek951kXTBzo.

A video showing station teaching: https://www.youtube.com/watch? v=DkY2D-f3JNo.

Targets for Co-Teaching Success: http://www.middleweb.com/22996/
3-targets-for-co-teaching-success-next-year/.

Seven Tips for Effective Collaboration: https://www.teachingchannel.
org/blog/2015/02/20/7-tips-for-collaboration/?utm_source=news
letter20150221.

CASE 9: WILL THEY CO-TEACH?

Mrs. Tyler has been teaching for twenty-eight years and is retiring in two
years. She has enjoyed teaching, but is looking forward to retirement and
being able to travel and spend time with her six grandchildren. She has
been teaching fifth grade for the past twenty years and enjoys the subject
matter. She also has all the materials and lesson plans in her file cabinet.
During the summer, a new principal was hired after the former principal
left unexpectedly.

Over the summer, the new principal called Mrs. Tyler to introduce
himself and invite her to a meeting. At the meeting, Mrs. Tyler was informed that she would have the special education cluster next year, including six students, and was told that she would be co-teaching reading
and language arts and math with a new teacher, Ms. Jones. Mrs. Tyler
informed the principal, Mr. Woodward, that she had not taught students
with disabilities for almost twenty years and inquired why those students could not go to another teacher. Why was she chosen? The principal assured her that Ms. Jones would help her with teaching the students
with disabilities.

Ms. Jones recently graduated from the local college and is excited to
be teaching in her hometown. In fact, Ms. Jones attended Parkside Elementary School herself. The principal explains that since Mrs. Tyler has
so much experience and such a good reputation as a teacher, he believes
this will be the perfect model for Ms. Jones. Mrs. Tyler shared that she
had always had the gifted students and that she had struggled teaching
students that had received special education services in the past. Mr.
Woodward informed her that she did not have any twice exceptional
students this year.

Mrs. Tyler left the meeting upset. She had her plans in place and had
worked hard over the years, and in the last two years of her career, she
did not feel that she should have something new. She called several
teacher friends and they told her that now she would be able to understand why they complained about all the extra meetings they had to
attend when they had students with disabilities in their classes. This
made her feel even worse. She worried that she would not enjoy the rest
of her summer.

The week before classes began, Mrs. Tyler and the other teachers re-
ported to Parkside to attend meetings and set up their classrooms. On the

first day, they had a faculty meeting and the new principal formally introduced himself and the new staff members, including Ms. Jones. Mrs. Tyler could not believe how young she was. Gosh, her grandchildren were almost her age.

After the meeting, Mrs. Tyler was talking with friends and Ms. Jones approached the group to introduce herself. Ms. Jones told the group that she was so excited to be teaching at the elementary school she attended and that she had great plans for the year. However, due to all the required meetings and training sessions, Ms. Jones and Mrs. Tyler could not meet until Friday. They agreed to meet at 10 a.m. on Friday.

Mrs. Tyler was still not happy to have another teacher to work with and to teach those students. With this group, their reputation preceded them and there were a lot of behavioral issues. Why was she assigned this group? She only had this year and next year to teach before retirement. She thought that Ms. Jones looked so young that the students would not listen to her. Furthermore, when she received her class list, she realized that she would not be teaching the gifted cluster this year.

On Friday morning, Ms. Jones came to Mrs. Tyler's room for the scheduled meeting. She hated that they had not planned for the first week of school earlier so she brought her computer with lots of activities bookmarked and saved. She wanted to contribute to the meeting and assure that the co-teaching relationship began well. She was eager to implement all the things she learned in her preservice program and student teaching.

As soon as she entered Mrs. Tyler's room, she noticed that the desks were neatly placed in rows. She also noticed that the textbooks were neatly stacked on each student's desk and that there were white bins at the back of the room labeled by subject. Each desk also had the student's names neatly written in cursive taped in the middle of the desks. She immediately remembered that it stated in several students IEPs that they could not read cursive writing. Ms. Jones felt that she was walking into her old elementary classroom.

During her practicum and student teaching, all the classrooms were arranged by groups or in a big horseshoe so the teacher could see each student and easily get to them. These arrangements also were conducive for group work. Also, she had not used textbooks often since most of the students she taught struggled with reading. She immediately realized that this was going to be a very different year. She had planned a lot of group activities for the first week, some involving technology, and she wondered how that would be received.

Ms. Jones liked to teach in groups and her behavior management system was based on points earned by the group. In her student teaching, she had divided the students into groups and given each group a name based on a common theme. Within each group she assigned each student a task such aa timekeeper, supply person, recorder, or presenter. This had always worked well and helped her students with disabilities interact socially.

The two teachers sat down at the back table and Ms. Jones had her students' IEPs so she could review them with Mrs. Tyler. Mrs. Tyler interrupted her and immediately informed her that she had to leave school early for a doctor's appointment so she would take the IEPs with her to review at home. On Monday, school would be starting and she proudly showed Ms. Jones her lesson plans. Mrs. Tyler also informed Ms. Jones that she would be teaching all week and provided her with copies of the lesson plans and worksheets.

Ms. Jones stated that she liked to get to know the students during the first week and build a classroom community so she had planned more interactive activities. Opening her laptop, she pointed to an activity that required students to bring five objects from home to share during classroom meetings. Mrs. Tyler interrupted and stated that she did not have classroom meetings. She was the teacher, there were a lot of academics to cover in fifth grade, and they needed to get started on the first day. She added that she did spend part of the first day going over when students were allowed to get out of their desks, the procedures for going to the pencil sharpener and the bathroom, and where they turned in work.

Mrs. Tyler pointed to bins with names of each subject for completed worksheets. She pointed to the worksheets and informed Ms. Jones that she had made her a copy of the materials so she could see what the students would be learning. She also gave her a copy of her lesson plans. Mrs. Tyler apologized and stated that she needed to get to her doctor's appointment and that she would see her on Monday. As she walked out, she said, "Don't worry, I have it all taken care of, all you need to do is show up. Have a good weekend."

Questions to Ponder

1. If you were Ms. Jones, what would you do? Develop a plan for implementation.
2. If you were Ms. Jones, which co-teaching model would you suggest to begin co-teaching with Mrs. Tyler?
3. In your opinion, do you think Mrs. Tyler is ready for the students with disabilities in her classroom?
4. Why do you think the principal selected these two teachers to work together?

Activities to Complete

1. Search for resources for co-planning.
2. Search for common issues and concerns teachers express about co-teaching. Brainstorm in class ways to deal with these issues.

3. Partner with another classmate and plan a lesson to be co-taught. Reflect on the process.

CASE 10: WHAT SHOULD MR. WALKER DO?

Mr. Walker has taught tenth grade for almost eight years now. He was actually hired the first year in October after the previous teacher left abruptly. He began as a long-term substitute and then was offered a contract in January. Those first couple years were the most difficult because he was teaching during the day on a provisional license and attending graduate school at night.

Mr. Walker had been a police officer prior to returning to school to become a teacher. His former coworkers could not believe that he was teaching and that he actually enjoyed working in the middle school. He was also a basketball coach and absolutely loved coaching and working with the students. Through coaching, he discovered that many students excelled in sports. He knew that sports were keeping a lot of students in school and that they would drop out otherwise. Over the years, he had worked hard to make learning fun in the classroom.

Mr. Walker teaches basic math and science classes and typically teaches the students who struggle in these areas. He loves technology and integrates technology and most recently game-based learning into his courses. His coaching experience showed him how much fun the students had playing games and the sense of collaboration and teamwork that developed throughout the season. Through past experiences he learned that creating a collaborative classroom environment helped build community and alleviate many behavior problems.

He attempted to create a fun, collaborative learning environment for the students. Both technology- and game-based learning proved to be ideal ways to differentiate instruction and he worked hard to create a collaborative rather than competitive environment. Through experience, he effectively differentiated instruction through technology. Before he used game-based learning and technology to individualize instruction, the students would often complain because they had to do more work than others in the class. Students were also more engaged and therefore behavior was less of an issue.

Mr. Walker was named Teacher of the Year at Los Angeles Middle School last year and because he had a reputation for working with the tough kids, he usually got the students with disabilities as well as the students who had extensive behavioral records. This year, Mr. Walker actually had the special education cluster in all four blocks he was teaching. It was November and he was wondering if earning Teacher of the Year was actually a curse. He felt that since he had a reputation for doing well with difficult students, that he had been given all of the difficult students.

This year, he taught two blocks of math and two blocks of science. Each block was a co-taught class and he was working with three different special educators. Over the past eight years, he had co-taught several classes, but not all four blocks. Previously, the most he had co-taught were two courses per year.

It was only November and he had already attended twelve IEP meetings, four Manifestation Determination Review meetings, in addition to his required meetings—the Professional Learning Community, department meetings, faculty meetings, and grade level planning meetings. To make matters worse, his planning block was different from two of the three co-teachers he taught with.

From day one, he had a great relationship with one teacher, Mrs. Wood, with whom he shared planning time. The two of them hit it off immediately and it was if they had taught together for years. He thought he had good co-teaching relationships in the past, but this was extraordinary. It was like having one brain between the two of them. They finished each other's sentences and their discipline policies were the same. It just really worked for both of them and the students were benefitting. Mrs. Wood had also embraced game-based learning and was always locating new resources to share.

However, with the other two special educators, things were much different. One of the teachers, Mrs. Delaney, was a seasoned special educator and was very knowledgeable, but she did not connect with the students. Mr. Walker thought of her as an old-school teacher and it reminded him of the way he had learned in school. In any classroom she taught, students were expected to sit in their seats and complete work. Of course, if they needed help or clarification, Mrs. Delaney was there to answer any questions. She would also work with students in small groups and do mini lessons in which she reviewed previously taught concepts or pre-taught new vocabulary and concepts.

Sometimes, Mr. Walker felt like one of her students because she constantly shared with him characteristics of students with disabilities. According to Mrs. Delaney, students with disabilities needed structure, constant repetition, and because she was responsible for documenting their goals, they needed to do a lot of paper and pencil work.

Mr. Walker and Mrs. Delaney did not seem to agree on anything when it came to teaching. Mr. Walker had overheard her talking to other teachers on more than one occasion about how chaotic and unstructured his classroom was. She had a lot more experience and specialized knowledge of working with students with disabilities and felt that it was her obligation to teach Mr. Walker as well as the students in his class. Mr. Walker knew that they were sending mixed messages to the students and that this was not good.

At this point, he wondered whose classroom it was anyway. Lately, Mrs. Delaney had begun pulling all of her students to the back table each block. In the small group, she taught new materials and reviewed previously taught concepts and then gave the students several worksheets to complete. At the small table with the students gathered around, she gave individualized help when students struggled. After all, this is what was called for in their IEPs and she was responsible for showing growth. However, in this block, there were eight students with IEPs, almost one-third of the class, and this was making it almost impossible for Mr. Walker to form groups. What was he going to do? He felt that he had lost control of his classroom.

Mr. Walker also worked with another special educator for two blocks of the day. He and this teacher, Mr. Toms, also had their differences. Mr. Toms was incredibly busy and Mr. Walker was not sure how he fit everything in. In addition to coaching football and soccer, Mr. Toms also held a part-time job at the local gym. By working at the gym, he got a free membership. Mr. Toms enjoyed working out and was training for an upcoming triathlon. He had a busy workout schedule that involved swimming or biking each morning and running and working out each evening. At the end of the day, as soon as the bell rang, he was off to the gym to work or to work out or was coaching. Mr. Walker had attempted to schedule a meeting with Mr. Toms on several occasions, but with his schedule, there just wasn't time.

Mr. Toms had never co-taught a class before and loved it. He scheduled all of his IEP meetings during this co-taught class and he did not have to find coverage. The policy at Los Angeles Middle was that if you held a meeting during the day, you had to find another teacher to cover your class. Of course everyone was busy and no one wanted to give up their planning to teach someone else's class. For Mr. Toms, this was the ideal situation.

Mr. Toms couldn't believe that he had never co-taught before. He was requesting next year to teach all of his classes this way. With his busy schedule, he never had time to make phone calls, grade papers, and write IEPs, but co-teaching allowed him to do all these things. After all, Mr. Walker was always there so it didn't matter if he came into class late or left a little early. By the time he got there on most days, the students were already on the computer or were in groups working so after a quick check-in, he could go to the back table and get to work.

However, Mr. Walker was not enjoying co-teaching with Mr. Toms. Not only was he doing all the work, but Mr. Toms was also asking him to make sure that all the athletes got passing grades. They needed a C or higher to be eligible to play on the sports teams. Mr. Toms knew that for many of these kids, sports would be their ticket out of the rough neighborhood and also it kept them out of the gangs. As a coach, he had to prepare them for high school football. That was when the college teams recruited. Most of the students were living in government housing and their families could not pay for college. After an especially difficult block, Mr. Walker had reached his limit. He asked Mr. Toms to stay so they could talk. He was at his limit and could not take it anymore!

Questions to Ponder

1. If you were Mr. Walker, what would you do? How would you approach the situations with Mr. Toms and Mrs. Delaney?
2. Considering it is November, are there things that Mr. Walker could have done differently in the first several months of school?
3. Do you think the students in each of Mr. Walker's classes may feel differently about each of the blocks based on the co-teaching arrangement? Describe how each group might be feeling.
4. What are the similarities and differences in each co-teaching arrangement? Why do you think these themes emerged?
5. Mrs. Delaney described being legally responsible for tracking student's academic progress and documenting their IEP goals. Is she correct that she needs paper and pencil methods to do this? How could the progress and documentation be done within the game-based learning and technology integration that Mr. Walker envisioned?

Activities to Complete

1. Pretend you are Mr. Walker. Develop a plan for working with Mr. Toms.
2. If you were Mr. Walker, develop a plan for working with Mrs. Delaney.
3. Prepare a lesson or a co-taught classroom in your subject area in which both teachers are actively involved in teaching the lesson. Indicate on the lesson plan, what each teacher is doing throughout the lesson.
4. Create a list of tasks that need to be completed weekly (grading, planning, gathering materials, etc.) to bring to a planning meeting so tasks can be assigned.
5. Make a list of statements from students in each of these co-taught classes. What are the similarities and differences?
6. At the beginning of the academic year, it is important to introduce both teachers. Develop an introduction for yourself, and working with a partner, an introduction to the class explaining what co-teaching is, why the class is taught in this manner, and what that will mean for the students in the class.

SIX

Working with Other Professionals

As the school year was ending, Mr. Waterman, assistant principal of Oak Grove Elementary School, asked Mrs. Arthur to come to his office. After she sat down, he congratulated her on nearly completing another successful second grade year. She thanked him, wondering what was coming next. As it turned out, his next words caused her to experience a very different aspect of education.

"We just learned that a new student has transferred into this district and will be joining us at Oak Grove next year. He has a fairly significant form of autism and will be included in a general second grade classroom for most of the day. I think that you would do a good job with him, and I would like to place him in your class next year. Will you accept?"

Mrs. Arthur thought a minute and then said, "I don't know anything about teaching students with autism. I have worked with students with learning disabilities and ADHD, and have collaborated with Ms. Thomas, the special education teacher, but autism seems like a very different challenge. I am a little uncertain."

Mr. Waterman reassured her. "You will have help from Ms. Thomas, and also from other professionals who work with this child. I know you can do it. The IEP meeting will be on Monday." After more consideration, Mrs. Arthur agreed to have the new student in her classroom. She decided that as she was entering her fifth year of teaching, she was ready for a new challenge.

As she entered the meeting room on Monday, Mrs. Arthur was surprised by the number of people in the room. She was used to having Ms. Thomas there, and Mr. Waterman and the parent, but there were several more professional-looking people, all unfamiliar to her. When introductions were made, she found out that the team working with Martin, the new student, consisted of an autism specialist, speech and language specialist, occupational therapist, physical therapist, and school counselor. She wondered what all these people did and how she would be able to coordinate Martin's educational program with all of them. It was the beginning of a new learning experience.

RELATED SERVICES

IDEA lists specific related services that must be available to a student with a disability who needs them (see textbox 6.1). Some of the services are more commonly provided than others. Early identification and assessment are required to be implemented for all children in each school division. Other services, such as social services and school health, are usually provided to all students, regardless of whether or not they have a disability.

Textbox 6.1
  Related Services
  Transportation
  Early identification and assessment of disabilities in children
  Speech-language pathology
  Audiology services
  Interpreting services
  Psychological services
  Parent counseling and training
  Physical and occupational therapy
  Recreation, including therapeutic recreation
  Social work services in schools
  School health services
  School nurse services
  Counseling services, including rehabilitation counseling
  Orientation and mobility services
  Medical services (only to diagnose or evaluate a child's disability)
  See more at http://www.wrightslaw.com/info/relsvcs.faqs.htm. #sthash.zo9gWNDj.dpuf.

Most of the related services are required to be provided only to students who have a disability. Speech and language can be a disability in itself, or the services can be provided as a related service. Orientation and mobility training is for students who are vision impaired and need assistance in learning how to move around the school safely. Interpretation services allow students with hearing impairments understand what is being said to them.

The most commonly provided related services in school settings are speech and language, occupational therapy, occupational therapy, and special transportation.

SPEECH AND LANGUAGE SERVICES

A speech and language pathologist works with students who have disorders of communication. The disorders can be divided into three categories:

1. Speech

   - Articulation—the production or pronunciation of specific sounds
   - Fluency—speech rhythm problems, such as stuttering
   - Voice—inappropriate pitch or harsh voice

2. Language

   - Syntax—using the correct parts of speech when speaking
   - Semantics—expressing meaning correctly when speaking
   - Pragmatics—the nonverbal aspects of communication, such as body language, conversational conventions, or turn taking

3. Language processing

   - Understanding language that is heard clearly

OCCUPATIONAL THERAPIST

An occupational therapist helps clients learn skills that assist with job related or daily living activities. In the case of a school student, it often takes the form of improving fine motor skills, helping students to access assistive technology, and assisting with sensory needs.

- Fine motor needs
  - Handwriting training
  - Correct positioning
    - Correct chair and desk size
    - Use of a slant board
    - Use of a cushion to improve posture
  - Ensuring that classroom lighting is appropriate
  - Training in eating and other aspects of self-care
- Assistive technology (AT)

- Working with AT specialist to determine appropriate technology
- Assisting with training for the student
- Determining correct positioning so that technology can be accessed

- Sensory needs

  - Providing items such as "wiggle cushions" and weighted vests to provide sensory feedback
  - Training students to fill their sensory needs
  - Educating teachers on the need for movement time, appropriate room arrangement, or snack breaks for students with sensory integration weaknesses

PHYSICAL THERAPY

Physical therapy is provided to students who have problems with gross motor movements (walking, jumping, running, carrying things) that interfere with their ability to navigate or participate fully in school activities. Their responsibilities include:

- Collaborate with teachers and other school personnel to modify the school and schedule to accommodate the student's physical needs

  - Change door knobs so that doors can be opened independently
  - Remove rugs to allow for walker movement
  - Arrange classroom furniture to allow for wheelchair movement
  - Allow sufficient time for slower movement from room to room

- Support the safe transportation of students

  - Ensure that the schedule includes time for movement to the bus
  - Monitor safety measures (seatbelt, wheelchair security) on the bus

- Familiarize students with the school environment

  - Practice walking or moving the wheelchair to classes
  - Practice carrying a cafeteria tray
  - Practice opening bathroom doors

- Assist with participation in physical education activities

- Advise teachers on methods to adapt activities to accommodate the student's needs
- Provide adaptive materials when necessary

- Select, modify, or customize adaptive equipment

  - Standing frame
  - Adapted desk

- Select, modify, or customize adaptive technology

  - Work with the AT specialist to determine appropriate technologies
  - Work with the occupational therapist to help the student access and use the technology
  - Monitor the effectiveness of the technology

Physical therapists, occupational therapists, and speech and language pathologists often work closely together, particularly when helping students use AT to communicate.

OTHER PROFESSIONALS

While these are the most common special professionals that work in school settings, there are others with whom a teacher may work as she includes students with different disabilities in her classroom.

Teacher of the Vision Impaired — Consults with teachers about presentation methods, classroom arrangement, or lighting; modifies materials; provides Braille and recorded materials; assists with movement throughout the school (orientations and mobility); and teaches the student strategies to enable him to learn, perform everyday activities, and participate in the general curriculum.

Teacher of the Hearing Impaired—Consults with teachers about classroom arrangement and effective presentation methods, assists with use of hearing aids or FM (frequency modulation) clarifying devices, teaches language skills (signing, reading, writing, speaking, etc.), teaches other academic skills as appropriate, coordinates interpreters, assists student with social interactions, and facilitates communication with parents.

Behavior Specialist—Consults with teachers, observes a student in different school settings, collects data on school behaviors, develops behavior plans in collaboration with teachers, assists with implementation, monitoring of behavior changes, and revision of plans.

Mrs. Arthur was introduced to all the related service providers at Martin's IEP meeting. She also met his mother, who was pleasant and cooperative, but was very clear on the type of program she expected for her son. Each of the service providers explained their reports and then recommended the goals and level of service that they proposed for Martin's second grade year.

The speech and language pathologist recommended classroom-based services for sixty minutes each week and pull-out services for ninety minutes each week. In the classroom she would focus on helping Martin follow directions and communicate with his teacher and classmates. In their individual pull-out sessions they would work on vocabulary development, communicating meaning clearly, and pragmatics.

The occupational therapist proposed delivering all classroom-based services. She would be in the classroom ninety minutes each week, helping Martin deal with his sensory integration problems through provision of a therapy ball for sitting and a sensory corner for him to use when he became overwhelmed. She would also help Martin complete fine motor tasks.

The physical therapist noted that Martin had completed nearly all of his gross motor goals. He was now able to move around the school safely and to engage in all of the physical activities he was likely to encounter in the school. She recommended that Martin receive only consultative services in the upcoming year. The physical therapist would communicate with the teachers, other therapists, and parents every two weeks to ensure that his progress continued. If necessary, changes could be made to the IEP at a later date to add more direct physical therapy services.

In addition, Ms. Thomas, the special education teacher, would be providing classroom-based services to Martin. She would provide instruction and support in the classroom each day for sixty minutes during the language arts period.

Mrs. Arthur had learned a lot in this IEP meeting. She now knew the four professionals who would be helping her teach Martin. But she was still concerned about how it would all work. Who would determine the schedules? How would they communicate with each other since the occupational therapist and the physical therapist worked at several schools? What if they asked her to do something for Martin that she thought would not be good for her other students? What if they disagreed on what was best for Martin? Wouldn't it be easier to just teach Martin herself?

TEAMING

As Mrs. Arthur saw at the IEP meeting, there are several types and levels of service that can be provided to a student. Each of these levels involves a different type of interaction with the classroom teacher. In addition, the therapists need to communicate with each other to provide the most effective services to Martin. Essentially, all of Martin's therapists, teachers, and his parents need to function as a team.

Each member of the team has a role, a specialty. The leader of the team is usually the special education teacher. She is the person who facilitates communication, coordinates feedback, monitors progress, and calls meetings to make any necessary changes in goals and service levels. She also focuses on classroom accommodations and the overall academic progress of the student.

While the specialists work to improve the student's performance in their particular area, it is also important that they keep the overall development in mind. The student's optimum growth may at times require that members move outside the boundaries of their traditional role.

One way to look at special educational teams is as multidisciplinary, interdisciplinary, or transdisciplinary:

Multidisciplinary teams consist of specialists who perform their different functions independently. They do their evaluations, develop their schedule, deliver their services, and monitor progress. They meet when necessary, usually at annual IEP meetings.

Interdisciplinary teams also perform their functions independently, but they meet more frequently to discuss progress, collaborate on program changes, and make schedule changes.

Transdisciplinary teams function as true teams. They keep the overall goal in mind (student progress), and willingly take on instruction or support that would traditionally belong to a different therapist. For example, a classroom teacher, after observing the occupational therapist working on letter formation, incorporates the technique into her daily instruction. Or a speech therapist may consult with the special education teacher about appropriate vocabulary to use in her therapy sessions. The roles are blended and shared. These transdisciplinary teams are the ideal (Friend, 2008).

As in most team situations, *clarity of goals* is key. In special education it is not difficult to establish the goal, as the focus of all efforts are on the progress of a particular student. At times, however, assessment data and role protection can blur that goal. Some teams place a picture of the student, or a sample of his work, in a prominent place during the meeting so that the true goal is not obscured.

A second key element of team success is *communication*. This can be particularly difficult in a school setting where daily schedules are highly structured and free time is scarce. When itinerant therapists are in different places before and after school, it is even more difficult. However, if the team is convinced that success depends on frequent contact, communication methods can be found. Use of video or audio technology, or even a notebook in which each member (including the parent) jots down session progress and asks questions of other team members are some ideas.

Mrs. Arthur knew she was in for a new experience when she agreed to include Martin in her classroom. She learned a great deal about the roles that each of the professionals played. Now she had to see if they could function as a true team focused on his progress when the school year began.

Websites

> The site also has other excellent fact sheets such as occupational therapy and UDL, Working with Teachers, and at: http://www.aota.org/-/media/Corporate/Files/AboutOT/Professionals/WhatIsOT/CY/Fact-Sheets/School%20Settings%20fact%20sheet.pdf.
>
> Fact Sheet on occupational therapy in schools: http://www.apta.org/uploadedFiles/APTAorg/Advocacy/Federal/Legislative_Issues/IDEA_ESEA/PhysicalTherapyintheSchoolSystem.pdf.
>
> Physical therapy in school settings: http://www.familyconnect.org/info/education/your-childs-educational-team-and-placement/central-role-of-the-tvi/235.
>
> The role of a vision teacher: http://www.familyconnect.org/info/education/know-your-rights/expanded-core-curriculum/235.
>
> Description of educational needs for a student with vision impairments: http://www.asha.org/policy/GL2004-00202/#sec1.2.
>
> Role of teacher of students with hearing loss: http://www.wrightslaw.com/info/relsvcs.faqs.htm#sthash.zo9gWNDj.dpuf.
>
> Interdisciplinary teams in schools: http://www.emstac.org/resources/teaming.pdf.
>
> Guiding the school counselor—IRIS module: http://iris.peabody.vanderbilt.edu/module/cou/#content.
>
> Assistive Technology—IRIS module: http://iris.peabody.vanderbilt.edu/module/at/#content.

CASE 11: WHERE IS THE TEAM?

Refer to the "Working with Other Professionals" section for more details on the beginning of this case.

When Martin arrived on the first day of his fourth grade year, Mrs. Arthur thought she was ready. With some difficulty, she had developed schedules with the occupational therapist, speech therapist, and special education teacher. It involved a reluctant change on her part, as she had to adjust her math period to accommodate the itinerant occupational therapist, who was only at the school in the late morning. Since Ms. Thomas, the special education teacher, was alternating between math and language arts, her schedule had to be changed as well.

In addition, Mrs. Arthur had placed Martin's desk in a place that she thought would have minimal distractions and had set up a "Quiet Corner" where he could go to relax. She imagined that things would go smoothly now that she and the other team members were prepared.

The reality was quite different. Martin was an unexpectedly large child. He was tall and overweight, and his clothes, although new and clean, looked sloppy on him. He was upset with his mother as they arrived because she would not stop for doughnuts on the way to school. She was distraught by his agitated behavior, but as she tried to calm him down, he pushed her away and said, "I don't like this new school."

Martin barely looked at Mrs. Arthur when she greeted him. Instead, he started circling the room, still claiming that he did not want to be in the new school. When he saw his name on his desk he sat in his chair, telling his mother to bring his backpack, which she was carrying. Together they put his materials in his desk and eventually he was calm enough to greet Mrs. Arthur under his mother's instruction and to explore the Quiet Corner.

As the other children began to arrive and his mother left, Martin sat in the Quiet Corner humming and looking at the ceiling.

When all the children arrived, Mrs. Arthur described a game they would play to help them get to know each other. She asked Martin to come back to his seat and he ignored her. When she went over and held out her hand, he turned away saying, "I want to stay here." Finally she asked another student to go invite Martin to join them, and he consented to move to his desk. He observed his classmates as they played the game, but he did not join in.

As the school year proceeded, Mrs. Arthur made the following observations about Martin: he could read fairly well, probably on an early second grade level. He refused to do very much writing. The work he did produce was disorganized and barely readable due to poorly formed letters. He was also weak in math, as he did not seem to have a good sense of number quantities, often confused plus and minus signs, and made calculation errors. Mrs. Arthur feared that it would be difficult for him to learn multiplication and division.

Martin's behavior was variable. On some days he was calm and fairly compliant unless he became frustrated with a writing or math assignment. On other days he entered the classroom upset and did little work all day. It was very difficult to motivate him to be productive on those days.

Socially Martin struggled as well. He rarely looked anyone in the eye. During free time and recess he would go toward groups of children, seeming to want to interact with them. However, such attempts usually ended up with tears or angry shouts. The children welcomed him at first, but Martin usually grabbed toys or used his size to be sure he started first or won the game. Mrs. Arthur tried to talk with him about his behavior, but it did not change.

Then there was his schedule. Mrs. Arthur thought she would go crazy at times. It seemed like every time she got involved in a lesson, one of the therapists was at the door. Whether whey came in to stay a while, or to take Martin for individual instruction, it was an interruption.

The specialists were definitely helpful at times. Ms. Thomas, who was there every day, got Martin to do some writing activities and suggested some good modifications on his math papers so that he was more successful. The occupational therapist set up a slant board on his desk that he liked, and added some materials to the Quiet Corner that seemed to help calm him down.

She was not sure what the speech therapist was doing. He needed help with his articulation, particularly the L and S sounds, and he surely needed to work on looking at people when he speaks and taking turns. When the speech therapist came into the room three times a week, she mostly sat and watched. When Martin returned from her pull-out sessions he was usually agitated and refused to do any work.

Mrs. Arthur never saw the autism specialist or the physical therapist. She assumed that they were talking with Ms. Thomas, but she had not heard anything about their conversations.

And then there was Ms. Carmichael. In November Ms. Thomas said that, due to an increase in her caseload, she was getting a paraprofessional to help her. Therefore, Ms. Carmichael would be coming into the classroom two of the five days each week in place of herself. Ms. Thomas said that she would supervise Ms. Carmichael, and that they would talk about Martin's progress every day.

Unfortunately, Ms. Carmichael appeared to have no training in teaching children. She had two basic approaches with Martin: either she pushed too forcefully to get him to complete work, or she did the work for him. There were a number of math papers with Martin's name on them that were completed in Ms. Carmichael's handwriting. All Mrs. Arthur's efforts to talk with Ms. Carmichael or Ms. Thomas about the situation resulted in very little change.

After three months of school, Mrs. Arthur was thoroughly frustrated. She had a soft place in her heart for Martin, who seemed so confused and desperate most of the time. And she thought that he was not getting the education he deserved. At the IEP meeting in the spring the group described themselves as a team working together to help Martin. But Mrs. Arthur felt more like a traffic controller than a team member. People came and went, but no one was working together. It felt like the responsibility for Martin's education was all on her shoulders.

Questions to Ponder

1. Write out Mrs. Arthur's schedule based on the services listed in the introduction and the details in the case. How do you think it could be improved?
2. List all the specific problems (related to each specialist) that Mrs. Arthur is facing. Rank them in the order of importance.
3. Describe what she should do to address the problems. What is the first thing you would do if you were Mrs. Arthur?
4. What do you think is in the Quiet Corner? What does it look like? How do you think Martin uses it for sensory fulfillment?
5. Describe a typical school day for Martin from his point of view. How do you think he is feeling about school? Is he happy there? What is he scared of?
6. What are the particular challenges of working with a paraprofessional? You will be supervising another adult as well as managing your students. How do you deal with the challenges?

Activities to Complete

1. Research other professional roles in schools and describe their functions.
2. Examine the IRIS module at http://iris.peabody.vanderbilt.edu/module/rs/ Note these particular sections:

   > Videos illustrating the work of speech therapists:http://iris.peabody.vanderbilt.edu/module/rs/cresource/q2/p05/#content
   >
   > Videos illustrating the work of occupational therapists:http://iris.peabody.vanderbilt.edu/module/rs/cresource/q2/p06/#content
   >
   > Videos illustrating the work of physical therapists:http://iris.peabody.vanderbilt.edu/module/rs/cresource/q2/p07/#content

   What did you learn from these videos? What surprised you?

3. On page 10 of the IRIS module at http://iris.peabody.vanderbilt.edu/module/rs is a list of other related services with links to IRIS explanations of these services. Look at these. Select two of them and describe how they would be helpful in situations you have experienced or seen in schools.
4. At the bottom of page 7 of the IRIS module at http://iris.peabody.vanderbilt.edu/module/rs/cresource/q2/p07/#contenta physical therapist reflects in an audio about what it means to work on a team. How do you think this applies to other related service providers? Do you agree that the classroom teacher is the team leader?

If so, what training does she need to fulfill this role? How does this understanding apply to Mrs. Arthur's situation?

5. Interview a related service provider who works with students with disabilities at school. Find out what she or he does. What training did he or she have? What are the biggest challenges? What are the most rewarding aspects of the job?

CASE 12: SHOULD EVELYN HAVE COME HOME?

Evelyn wanted to come home. She was starting her freshman year and she wanted to attend high school with her brother Ricky, who would be a junior. Her parents agreed and then contacted the school to get it arranged. They knew it would be complicated.

Evelyn had been profoundly deaf since birth. Starting in third grade, she had been attending the state school for the deaf and blind (SDB). It was about two hours from her home; she lived there during the week and came home on the weekends.

The school had been a good place for her. She became adept at using sign language, and was able to interact easily with her friends and teachers there. For many years she had been happy learning in the comfortable atmosphere of the residential school. She had some local friends whom she had met in primary school, and continued to see them occasionally on weekends. She sometimes went to parties with Ricky and his friends. Since Ricky was also an adept signer, he could act as an interpreter for her.

For two main reasons, it seemed time to come back to the local high school. One was academic. Evelyn was fortunate—her family learned to sign when she was a child and so she has had a full language experience throughout her development. However, that was not true for many of her classmates at the state school. Many of them had delayed sign language acquisition and, as a result, were delayed in their development of reading and writing skills. Evelyn wanted to take the challenging English and math courses that were not offered at the state school.

The other was social. Evelyn knew that, while the state school was comfortable, it was not reality. She wanted to experience the high school social scene that she had seen through her brother's experiences. Even though she would have difficulty communicating with her classmates, she thought that it would be worth the additional stress.

After Evelyn's mother contacted the high school, a meeting was set up with a district special education administrator, two of the freshman class teachers, the assistant principal, and Evelyn and her mother, who served as an interpreter.

The administrators expressed surprise that Evelyn wanted to return, since they had expected her to remain at the state school until graduation.

Ms. Butler, the special education administrator, said that she believed that Evelyn was getting a good education at SDB, and she was concerned that it would be hard to replicate the same level of services at the local high school. She did note, however, that the law required that services be provided in the location closest to the student's home school, so they would find a way to make it successful.

The meeting began with a consideration of the type of services that would be necessary for Evelyn to have access to the curriculum:

1. A sign language interpreter who would be with her throughout the school day, including after school activities if necessary;
2. Services from a speech therapist;
3. Services from a deaf and hard of hearing resource teacher (who would act as the team leader);
4. Services from an AT specialist to ensure that Evelyn had access to closed captioning whenever needed.

Since qualified interpreters are difficult to find, the district administrator knew that she would have to begin searching immediately. The remaining specialists were already employed by the school division, so they could add Evelyn to their caseload. An IEP meeting would be scheduled near the end of the summer so that each of the specialists could develop goals for Evelyn.

One of the teachers at the meeting was Mr. Hudson, who taught English. He was impressed by Evelyn's composure among the adults and her determination to do well at Mountain High School. But he wondered how well she would respond in class or work in groups with the other students. He hoped that her reading and writing abilities were on a ninth grade level.

By the middle of the summer, the special education administrator, Ms. Butler, had still not found an interpreter. Some people had responded to her job posting, but they did not have the necessary qualifications. She knew that Evelyn's interpreter would have to have the highest level of certification to facilitate her success in high school. Finally, out of desperation, she hired Olivia Michaels.

Ms. Michaels was a college graduate who had not yet completed her training to become a certified American Sign Language interpreter. Her records showed that she had completed approximately half of the program. She had had some experience interpreting at an elementary school, but had never worked with a high school student. Ms. Butler hired Ms. Michaels on a temporary basis, resolving to keep looking for a more qualified person.

At the IEP meeting, Evelyn met all of the teachers she would have that year. Together with the speech therapist, deaf and hard of hearing specialist, and assistive technology specialist, they developed goals for Evelyn. Evelyn's mother was there, but Ms. Michaels acted as the interpreter.

The team members learned that it was important to speak directly to Evelyn rather than to the interpreter.

The school year started off well. Evelyn's teachers learned that while her background was slightly delayed, she worked hard and was quickly catching up with her peers. Mike, the AT specialist, had installed closed captioning on the computer in the classroom and was looking into computer-assisted note-taking systems.

The resource specialist met with Evelyn before school twice a week to make sure everything was going according to the plan. Evelyn met with the speech therapist during her study hall period to help her develop ways to communicate with her friends. Texting was very helpful, and she was gaining skill in reading lips and facial expressions. The team communicated via email faithfully once every two weeks.

The problem was Ms. Michaels, the interpreter. At first she seemed fine, as Evelyn could understand her signs well and she appeared to be communicating all the information from the teachers. But Mr. Hudson, in particular, began to have concerns. He believed that Ms. Michaels was exceeding the parameters of her job. Instead of focusing on translating the teacher's and students' words for Evelyn, she often communicated with her at other times. He didn't know if they were talking about the assignment (was Ms. Michaels giving Evelyn the answers?) or about unrelated topics. Either one seemed inappropriate to Mr. Hudson. He believed that the interpreter was acting more like one of his students than a professional in the classroom.

Questions to Ponder

1. What should Mr. Hudson do? Who should he talk to first about his concerns? Who is responsible for dealing with problems with the interpreter?
2. What if Evelyn says that she likes Ms. Michaels and does not want her replaced because they are now friends? What is the responsibility of her educational team?
3. What is the best outcome for this case? How can that be achieved?
4. Do you think that the team of related service professionals are acting appropriately? How could they do even better?
5. What would happen if the speech therapist became ill and no replacement was found to work with Evelyn? What are the legal responsibilities of the school district?

Activities to Complete

1. Research the role that speech therapists should play when working with students who are deaf and hard of hearing. Describe two hypothetical students who are deaf or hard of hearing at different

levels or with different types of skills. Write five IEP goals for each one that might be addressed by a speech and language therapist.

2. Research the technology advances that are being made for students who are deaf and hard of hearing. What might Evelyn's related services look like in two or three years?

3. What related services would be required by a student who is blind? Write a case describing a student who is blind returning from the state school for the deaf and blind. What related services would he require?

SEVEN

The Effective Classroom

Classrooms are complicated places. Each moment of the school day involves multiple interactions among students, teachers, other adults, curriculum demands, learning materials, and schedules. Organizing and managing these interactions is a daunting task, and when the system fails to perform well, students suffer. Some students suffer more than others.

When a student becomes a "behavior problem," teachers tend to believe that the problem lies within the student. He may be referred for a special education evaluation to determine if there is some type of disability causing the problem. Seldom do teachers look to see whether the "disability" rests with a classroom that fails to provide the type of support the student needs.

While some students may be able to survive in a poorly organized classroom, others lack the internal organization necessary to move forward on their own. Very few students actually thrive.

So what does this well-functioning classroom look like?

CREATE A CLASSROOM COMMUNITY

A well-functioning classroom is a community. Students help each other, respect each other's ideas, collaborate with each other, and care for each other. But this does not happen automatically. The community is developed through intentional actions on the part of the teacher. The Responsive Classroom program (Chaney, 2002) is one example of a system that helps teachers establish a collaborative classroom in which students interact, communicate, learn, and become independent.

Programs such as the Responsive Classroom are based on the premise that time used at the beginning of the year to help students know and appreciate each other is well spent. Teachers learn about their students as well, and they can use that knowledge to tap into student strengths and interests when the tasks become challenging. Activities such as sharing backgrounds, playing games, learning routines, and practicing how to handle difficult emotional situations give students new understandings and skills and also provide a shared understanding of expected behaviors.

USE SPACE THOUGHTFULLY

Each aspect of the physical space (furniture, materials, desks, chairs, etc.) is thoughtfully arranged. The arrangement should prompt the students to use the space appropriately. For example, if you want students to indicate their lunch choices as soon as they walk into the classroom, then make sure the lunch chart is right by the door. If they should pick up a warm-up assignment at first, place those papers by the door as well.

Mrs. Wright was frustrated because her kindergarten students kept wanting to sit in the adult rocking chair. She had to continually tell them to get off it during free time. She herself did not sit in it at any time, but she thought that it looked good in the classroom. She believed that the students were being obstinate and refusing to listen to her. When an observer suggested that she remove the chair, she was surprised. She had never considered that the problem was her classroom and not the students. When the chair was removed, a major source of conflict was also removed.

The way in which desks are arranged can also contribute to the atmosphere in a classroom. Desks in rows facing forward facilitate attention on the teacher, desks facing each other facilitate group work, and desks in a large circle facilitate whole-group discussion. The configuration of the desks also provides a reminder to the student as to which behaviors are expected. With training and practice, students can rearrange the space themselves as learning tasks demand.

Classroom teachers use wall space in many ways. Word walls, reminding posters, and displays of student work are evident everywhere. However, it is essential that the walls are not too crowded and that the space is used intentionally. Visual prompts are very effective, but a punctuation poster can become invisible to the students if it is one of twelve other posters that stay in the same place all year.

Thoughtful teachers take advantage of the fact that novelty attracts attention by highlighting certain lists or posters and by adding and removing displays often. Wall space is a valuable asset since information presented visually is usually more meaningful and memorable to students than is information they hear. An effective teacher uses it well.

When a classroom is not functioning well—if students seem impulsive, unfocused, and unproductive, look to the physical arrangement of the room. Often adjustments in the space can make a big difference.

DEVELOP ROUTINES

Consistent routines provide much-needed structure for students. The routines also free up time spent in giving reminders and redirecting stragglers. In a well-functioning classroom students know the expected way to do such things as ask permission to use the restroom, gain access to materials, transition to different subjects or activities, and even to indicate that they want to answer a teacher's question.

Students not only know the routines, they follow them consistently. At the beginning of the year the teacher introduces the procedures and the students practice them several times. There is a well-understood consequence for failing to follow the routines, and it is imposed fairly.

If one routine is not providing the expected smooth result, the teacher takes responsibility for figuring out the glitch. Is it too complicated? Does the classroom arrangement interfere with the routine? Do students need more practice? Sometimes the students can pinpoint the problem. The identified issues are addressed until the routine fulfills its function of ensuring a safe, orderly, productive classroom.

ANTICIPATE PROBLEMS

If you asked a teacher to identify problem times, areas, or students, you would likely get a prompt answer such as, "My students just don't know how to enter the classroom quietly," or "Mary takes forever to start a writing assignment," or "This group always gets in trouble in the lunch room," or "The students groan every time we take out the science books." In most classrooms there are certain issues that plague the teacher and the students every day. One common reaction is to blame the students: to complain that they are not taught well at home, that Billy gets everyone riled up, or that it is just a tough group this year.

But by concentrating on these problem areas and using pre-correction techniques to deal with them before they occur, teachers can often smooth out the rough spots. Teaching students the routines for beginning class each day, rehearsing and providing reminders, and ensuring that they are rewarded in some way for following the routine can take care of the morning hassle. The reward can be no more than saying "thank you" to random students at first. Eventually, the peaceful class beginning will be enough reward.

Anticipating which assignments might challenge certain students is part of a teacher's job. If Mary has difficulty beginning writing assignments, provide her with a list of steps to follow and help her become familiar with the steps. Other solutions might be to have her draw her thoughts out before writing, or working with a partner on writing assignments. Such anticipatory behavior on the part of the teacher replaces the repeated reminders to "get going," and helps to create a much more positive classroom atmosphere.

Pre-correction can help with the lunchroom problem. It is unlikely that hoping that things improve, or scolding students after they return from a chaotic lunch will change things. But modeling and role playing proper lunchroom practices, reiterating the rules before they leave the room every day, and reviewing their behavior after they return will make a difference. It can be done in a positive, even humorous way that instills pride and a sense of community in the students.

If the science book is too boring, put it aside and use experiments, videos, and trade books to teach the subject. Not only are you anticipating and solving the problem of the student groaning, you are also paying attention to student communication. Clearly, the boring text is not teaching them anything, so your instructional goals need to be met in another way.

USE PROMPTS

Prompts are a part of life. We use them all the time ourselves: a grocery list, a street sign, a touch on the elbow to remind someone move aside, a nod to encourage a friend to continue telling her story. We use them in classrooms as well: the alphabet chart over the chalkboard, a raised hand to ask students to line up outside, a clapping or counting routine to get students' attention.

The teacher in an effective classroom makes extensive use of prompts in a very conscious way. One important value of prompts is that they are a succinct (often nonverbal) way to control student behavior. Teachers do a lot of talking throughout the day. It is best when that talking is spent mainly on instruction, with behavioral issues being controlled through routines and prompts.

It would be a good exercise to spend a day looking at the prompts you use and determining how well they work. Do students ever look at the math problem-solving poster on the wall? What would be a better prompt to help them solve math word problems? How could you introduce a new prompt and evaluate how well it is working?

Mr. Anderson had always been fairly successful at gaining his high school English students' attention by raising his hand and waiting. But it didn't seem to work very well with this group. He decided that they needed a more dramatic prompt. So one evening he painted a red circle on the floor in a front corner of the room.

He refused to answer questions about the circle as the students entered the next day, but when they were seated and quiet he described its purpose. He said that no one was allowed in the circle, and that even he wouldn't stand in it unless he had something important to say. When he did stand there, he expected that they would immediately quiet down and listen. He asked them to converse with each other and then he stepped into the circle.

When they immediately became attentive, he told them that in recognition of the new procedure they wouldn't have any homework that night. He knew that the pairing of such good news with the prompt would make it more likely that they would pay attention the next time. He continued to use it to impart good news as often as possible, and the students were quick to listen when he entered the circle. Eventually it became a habit for them, and good news as well as bad could be delivered from the circle.

Students can also be taught to use nonverbal methods to prompt teacher behavior. Effective systems have been developed to inform the teacher about a student's level of comfort with an individual assignment. A stack of cups colored red, yellow, and green are placed on a student's desk. If the student is having no trouble with the work, he keeps the green cup on top. Yellow indicates that he is having difficultly but he is managing, and red is a signal that he needs help. When students use this method, much of the hand waving, head lowering, and even disruptive behavior can be avoided.

These examples show that prompts can be very powerful, but they need to be taught to the students and then constantly evaluated. Sometimes prompts, particularly visual ones, can become part of the background and be easily ignored. They may need to be refreshed, moved to a new position, or redesigned. Other times a familiar prompt continues to give students and teachers a useful way to communicate in a smoothly running classroom.

TEACH SCHOOL BEHAVIOR

It is the teacher's responsibility to teach students how to behave in school. Ideally, students would come to school able to act perfectly in each situation, but this is not the case. Some students have never been in school-like situations, and others need reminding over and over. The teacher in an effective classroom knows this. She knows that she will have to teach her students how she wants them to act in her classroom and that if she takes time to do this, her year will go much more smoothly.

As in the case of academic skills, students differ in their grasp of social skills. Some students may be reluctant to engage with classmates while others spend too much time socializing. Some students may be compulsive about organizing materials and finishing work quickly, while others seem scattered and slow in completing assignments. Reviewing these and other school behaviors at the beginning of the year provides a background for discussing issues when they arise later on.

One very effective way to teach behavior is through role playing. If, for example, you notice that students are consistently failing to clean up the art or computer space, you might set aside time for a reminder session. It can start with a role play by students or teachers imitating the wrong behavior in an exaggerated and humorous manner. Following a discussion, a second group can demonstrate the proper clean-up behavior. The next step might be practicing the clean-up steps and the process of evaluating how well the job has been done.

While some students need little more than reminders or group role play sessions to change their behavior, others are needier. If a student consistently ends up in tears after a few minutes of playground activity, he may require individual instruction from you on how to interact with his classmates. Following the instruction, practice, debriefing, and rewards for successes can ensure that he has learned new social skills.

HOLD EVERYONE ACCOUNTABLE

Taking responsibility as a teacher does not mean that the students are not to be held accountable for their behavior. No one learns or grows if they are allowed to break the classroom rules or fail to complete work without consequences (Linson, 2014).

If the classroom management plan (the contract between the students and teachers) states that "time out" is a consequence for a certain infraction, then the consequence needs to be imposed consistently. It works best if you regard the behavior not as a personal affront to you, but as a slip on the part of the student that will not be repeated once the consequence is experienced.

If you find that some students do not change their behavior after experiencing the consequence, the answer is not to let the behavior slide, but to dig into the problem. Does he need a different consequence? Does he need more support in performing the behavior? He learns nothing and the whole classroom suffers if you fail to hold him accountable.

This applies to academic behaviors as well. Even though Mary needs extra help getting started on the writing assignment, she must complete the assignment. It is easier on everyone, even the teacher, if she can get away with expending minimal effort, but she will not learn to persevere nor will she become a better writer. She needs to know that she will receive the help she needs, and perhaps the assignment will be altered for her, but she will be required to complete it to your satisfaction.

Consistency is key. Again, it may take time at the beginning of the year, but making it clear to students that you expect appropriate behavior and their best work each day is essential. You also make it clear that you will do your part by providing interesting, thorough instruction and a calm, orderly place to work.

BE PERSISTENT

As with many aspects of the effective classroom, the key is the attitude of the teacher. If a situation in the classroom is troublesome, the effective teacher believes that it is his responsibility to change it. He knows that he can make the change if he analyzes the problem carefully, develops a plan that may involve teaching new behavior to students, altering the classroom arrangement, developing a new prompt, or changing a teaching technique. He then carries out the plan, monitors its effectiveness, and makes modifications as necessary. He never throws up his hands, believing that the students are the problem and that there is nothing he can do about it.

We expect students to be persistent. When they struggle to learn, we are critical if they give up too easily, try to avoid work, or blame someone else for their problem. We know that the only way that they will succeed is by continuing to try even though it is difficult. As teachers we must model this persistence. When a student or classroom situation becomes problematic, effective teachers persist in seeking a solution.

Additional Resources

> Describes the principles of the Responsive Classroom program and provides information on trainings and resources: www.ResponsiveClassroom.org.
> Provides an overview of Michael Linsin's classroom management ideas with options for a weekly newsletter and other resources: http://www.smartclassroommanagement.com/about-smart-classroom-management/.

CASE 13: WHAT DOES AN EFFECTIVE CLASSROOM LOOK LIKE?

Rachel Goetz is a middle school math teacher. Her school has a diverse demographic and is in a very large city. She is known in her school as being an organized, effective teacher. Her principal, Mark, said that when he is tired of observing struggling teachers and wants to remember how teaching is supposed to look, he heads for Ms. Goetz's classroom. It is always a calm, productive place in which the students thrive.

Several principles guide Ms. Goetz's teaching behaviors: connections, independence, responsibility, choice, frequent assessment, and variety.

CONNECTIONS

Ms. Goetz makes a conscious effort to get to know her students. She calls each of the families early in the school year with positive information and continues to communicate with families throughout the year. She maintains a friendly, matter-of-fact manner with students and looks for opportunities to speak with them individually or in groups about their lives outside of school. "Smiley cards," delivered privately, lets students know when she appreciates something they do in class.

She also believes that students need opportunities to connect with each other. She expects that nearly every day will include some form of group or partner work. To make this work be successful, she assigns student to year-long "study teams" and she spends time at the beginning of the year teaching them to work together.

Last year she hit on a successful way to do this. She asked a group of her previous year's students to come to her classroom after school to help her. Together they created a video illustrating the ways in which she expected her students to cooperate in partner and group work. Her routines, behaviors, and interactions were clearly acted out by the older students.

At the beginning of the year she used the video to introduce her new students to the behaviors she expected, and showed it again later if they appeared to be forgetting. Ms. Goetz realized that there were several benefits to this type of video. A basic visual sample of the expected behaviors was very useful, but perhaps even more useful were the models provided by the upper classmen. A third benefit was the way that the video freed her up to watch student responses. Some students had definitely experienced similar expectations in their previous classrooms, but for others this type of formal group work was new for them. She would take these experience levels into account when she formed the groups.

INDEPENDENCE

Ms. Goetz says that she wants to have an organized classroom so that students can be independent in the small things. When students smoothly manage such things as materials, seating, and interactions on their own, she can teach instead of "putting out fires."

She has many ways of achieving this goal. Materials are well organized and students are assigned the tasks of managing delivery, collection, and clean-up. Students are trained to rearrange the desks quickly when necessary for group work or other activities. A map of the different arrangements is displayed, and each arrangement has a specific name. Groups of four is the "small dinner table" and three long rows of desks is the "big dining table." In this arrangement she sits with the middle group and can monitor each of the side groups as they tackle different assignments.

For each lesson she creates a "Tool Kit" consisting of an explanation of the concept with diagrams, computation procedures, notes, reminders, and any specific materials needed. If a student is absent, she will say, "We missed you yesterday. It is your responsibility to check the Tool Kit so that you can participate in the lesson today." Students who did not miss a lesson but who failed to master the lesson may also choose to make use of the Tool Kit.

When independent work is assigned, she will ask, "Who believes they understand this well enough to be a resource for those needing reminders?" She then puts the names of the volunteers on the board so that they can be consulted by students who require help.

RESPONSIBILITY AND CHOICE

Students in Ms. Goetz's class are responsible for their learning and for their behavior. She provides support for both, but she makes it clear that they determine the outcome. They are expected to use the Tool Kit to learn what they missed through absences, and to find help from classmates or Ms. Goetz if confusion remains.

If behavior becomes an issue at some point, Ms. Goetz might say, "I will be calling your parents on Friday. You determine what the conversation is going to be about." The student knows that the conversation with his parents will occur, but that if he takes on the responsibility of becoming more cooperative, it will be one of Ms. Goetz's positive contacts.

Periodically, Ms. Goetz will declare a "What Do You Need?" day. This is essentially a review day, with students deciding for themselves which areas of the curriculum have challenged them. She forms groups focusing on different skills and concepts, and students attend the one they believe fits their needs. One group is called "Push Me," designed for students who want to be challenged on a particular topic. The special day is announced earlier so that students have time to consider their weak areas.

Not surprisingly, there are still students who say they don't know which group to join. To continue to promote individual responsibility, Ms. Goetz will give these students a choice between two suggested groups, or ask them to identify the lowest grade they had the previous week to determine their needy area.

FREQUENT ASSESSMENT

To continue to promote independence and responsibility, Ms. Goetz teaches students to self-assess their understanding and their work. She uses exit slips, asking students to describe how well they understood the lesson of the day. The required responses vary—written descriptions, a numerical rating, or circling the most appropriate descriptor.

The exit slips are also used to get information on students' level of engagement. She might ask them to rate their engagement from one to five, or to describe their engagement in one word. This type of assessment is also a rating of her own lesson, and she uses it to modify the way she teaches. A planning document helps her to record students' responses to the lessons for future reference.

Ms. Goetz uses the students' ratings of their own work to continue to teach them to monitor their performance and to challenge themselves. For example, when she offers differentiated assignments, she describes which tasks she considers to be the most and least challenging. If a student chooses an easier task, she might say to her, "I see that you rated your understanding of this concept as a 5. Why didn't you choose this more challenging assignment?"

VARIETY

Ms. Goetz believes strongly in the importance of variety in her instruction. She knows that novelty increases student engagement and makes learning pleasurable. Recently she made videos of herself demonstrating two different methods for doing a multiplication task. She played the videos and then led the students in a debate over which method they thought was best. The procedure demanded that they analyze and learn both methods, verbalize their thinking regarding the usefulness of each method, and engage in discussion with their classmates. And it was fun.

She has found that videos illustrating mathematical procedures work well in several ways. The instruction is done automatically, freeing her up to check in with students while it is playing. She can also post the video on the class website so that they can refer to it when doing homework.

Working in groups or with partners, debating, choosing which differentiated assignment to complete, responding to assignments through different modalities—Ms. Goetz continually finds ways to change her instruction. She says, "I don't want to just tell them." Instead, she brings in active, interesting, challenging methods that enable students to bring their minds, and emotions, to math class.

Questions to Ponder

1. This is an example of an actual classroom, and Ms. Goetz is a real teacher. She clearly has figured out how to implement most of the basic aspects of good teaching. What do you think are the biggest challenges related to teaching this way?
2. Choose two or three of the methods used by Ms. Goetz in her math class and describe how they could be used in another middle or secondary subject area, such as English or chemistry.
3. Do you think Ms. Goetz's classroom would be a good place for a student with an emotional disability? Why or why not? What types of supports might he need? Answer the same questions for a student with a learning disability, mild autism, and a mild intellectual disability.
4. Ms. Goetz usually has a student teacher, and she finds ways to get other adults into her classroom. What is the best way for her to use these adults? What challenges are involved in utilizing extra adults in a classroom?

Activities to Complete

1. Observe a middle or high school math class. Compare the methods you see used with some of those described in this case. Which do you think will be most effective?
2. Write a script for one of the phone conversations Ms. Goetz might have with a parent at the beginning of the year. How will Ms. Goetz begin the conversation? What will she say about the student and about her program? How do you think the parent will respond? You might write two scripts—one for a successful conversation and one for one that is not very successful.
3. Do you think teaching is fun? Why? Interview three teachers and find out what they think about the pleasures of teaching.

CASE 14: DOES RODNEY HAVE A DISABILITY?

Mrs. Allen's Classroom

On a Monday morning in November, Mrs. Allen got a new student in her kindergarten class. Rodney arrived early with his mother, dressed neatly and with an eager look on his face. His mother told the teacher that they had recently moved to the city after spending several years in a rural area. When questioned, she said that Rodney had not gone to any preschool, but that he had always been a talkative boy and interacted well with his extended family.

Mrs. Allen was proud of her classroom management skills. Her students knew the rules and generally behaved according to the teacher's expectations. Because she believed in the importance of strong language skills, she spent much of the day having students listen to picture books, retell stories, and share events from their lives. They generally talked to the whole group, as individual conversations were prohibited. Some children had difficulty sitting still on the story rug, but most of them were able to settle in well by this point in the school year.

Rodney was a clear exception. He could not sit still on the rug or anywhere. He seemed to be in constant motion. He loved playing on the playground with other students, but he was frequently more aggressive than they were. He never hurt anyone, but he often sat in time out for yelling or grabbing. His classmates liked being with him because he was exciting, but they remained wary of him.

When Mrs. Allen tested Rodney, she learned that he could identify letters and numbers, and appeared to have a good sense of quantity. She was not surprised that he had little knowledge of letter sounds since he had not been to preschool. But his oral language skills did surprise her.

It seemed to her that the child could not talk straight. When he was asked to tell about his day, his narrative was completely disjointed. He went off on tangents about who was in his family and what he had done weeks ago. He could not begin to retell a story he had heard or relate events from his experience in a correct sequence. He could not listen to a story read by the teacher or told by another student without jumping up and adding ideas of his own.

Mrs. Allen decided that the best way to get Rodney into shape was to keep him as still and quiet as possible. She gave him negative consequences, including calls to his home, if he got out of his seat or if he neglected to raise his hand before speaking. She didn't let him tell any stories since they were so disjointed. Instead, she urged him to listen to other students to see how it should be done.

After five weeks she was at her wit's end. She saw no change in Rodney's behavior or language and she started to believe that he had a disability. Her punishments did not seem to have any effect—it seemed that he just couldn't help himself. Perhaps he had ADHD, a language disability, or even a form of autism. Whatever it was, he did not belong in her classroom. He was too disruptive.

The Referral

The first step in any referral for special education at the school was the Student Assistance Team (SAT): a group of teachers, guidance counselor, and an administrator. Before bringing a student to the team, the teacher had to talk with the parents, collect work samples and assessment results, and have another teacher observe the student. Mrs. Allen had samples of

Rodney's assessments and work, but she needed the other two requirements.

When Mrs. Allen spoke to Rodney's mother, she was not helpful. She said that Rodney was fine at home. He played well with his cousins and spoke very appropriately at the family gatherings. Everyone could understand him. He didn't seem to be any more active than anyone else.

She asked Mrs. Johnson to observe Rodney. She was a newer kindergarten teacher who was also on the SAT team. While Mrs. Johnson was in his classroom, Rodney displayed his usual active, loud behavior. Mrs. Allen was sure that Mrs. Johnson could see what a problem he was to her. She was more and more convinced that he had some type of disability.

At the SAT meeting, Mrs. Allen presented the information she brought on Rodney. She was hoping that she could make the case that a full evaluation should be recommended so that the process would not be delayed any longer. However, Mrs. Johnson surprised her. She said that based on her observation, Rodney was a normal kindergartner.

She believed, though, that he was in the wrong classroom. She wanted the chance to teach Rodney herself. The team agreed that a change in classrooms would be the first intervention tried for Rodney. If the problems persisted, he would be referred for a full evaluation.

Mrs. Johnson's Classroom

Mrs. Johnson's room was an entirely different place. It was orderly but in a very different way from Mrs. Allen's. At first glance it looked a little chaotic. There were centers set up with science experiments, math manipulatives, headphones, and writing implements. There was a couch in the corner. There were round tables with nametags at each place and plants in the middle.

Because Mrs. Johnson had spent several days at the beginning of the year modeling and practicing routines, the students' behavior was very orderly. They knew the procedures for entering the room, listening carefully, working at centers, and talking with their table partners. Mrs. Johnson believed that students learn best through talking, so she gave many opportunities for her students to discuss ideas with their partners. Under her guidance they had practiced holding productive conversations that followed the topic and ensured everyone's participation.

After her observation, Mrs. Johnson knew that Rodney was not yet ready to participate fully in her classroom. After all, he had missed the first weeks of modeling and practice. When she introduced the new student to the class she noted this, and asked for the students' help in making Rodney comfortable with his new classmates.

She assigned a capable student as his partner, and she herself monitored his language progress and center concentration carefully. She asked her assistant to stay near him during center and free play time, intervening with modeling and role playing when necessary.

Her actions were based on the belief that Rodney needed teaching, not punishment. He needed opportunities to try out the use of new language patterns rather than staying quiet. He needed a safe place to learn that words could get him what he wanted better than grabbing could. Her room was a place where these skills could be taught and practiced.

It didn't happen quickly, but Rodney did change. He learned that the form of communication that worked well with his family was not always appropriate in school. His new abilities to listen, express himself in a more linear way, and keep his body still at times helped him to become a success in school.

Questions to Ponder

1. Did Rodney have a disability? If not, what were the issues that caused the problems?
2. How were they resolved?
3. Do you think it was better to solve Rodney's problems through a classroom change rather than finding him eligible for special education? Why?
4. Would Mrs. Allen's classroom be a better place than Mrs. Johnson's for some students? Describe these students.
5. What do you think of the policy that a student had to be observed before coming to the SAT meeting? Why?

Activities to Complete

1. Write the story from the point of view of Rodney's mother. What did she make of his first experiences in school?
2. Look at the article on communication patterns athttp://www.lpi.usra.edu/education/lpsc_wksp_2007/resources/elliott.pdf. What do you think? How do you think it applies to Rodney's situation? How do you think it applies to education in general?
3. Do you think that Rodney should have worked with a speech and language pathologist? What goals might she have written? Don't forget that speech and language pathologists also work on pragmatic skills.
4. Interview an elementary principal and ask about the policies related to placing students in classrooms. How much consideration is given to matching student characteristics with teaching styles?

EIGHT

Behavior Management

FOUNDATION

The guidelines for applying discipline procedures to students with disabilities has been described as a "dual discipline" system, paralleling the system used for students without disabilities. However, when approached from a different viewpoint, the rules described in IDEA (2004) can be seen as a model that can be useful for all students.

The foundation of IDEA is a belief that all students are entitled to FAPE. This guarantee cannot be denied for any reason, not even if the student does not seem to deserve the education. The discipline rules are based on this foundation, as they specify that students with disabilities must be taught how to behave, supported as they learn behavior skills, not punished for behaviors that they cannot control, and never denied an education no matter how bad their actions are. However, the law also says that these students be removed from the general school population if they are a threat to others.

Another aspect of FAPE is the requirement that each student with disabilities be educated in the environment that is closest to the general population as possible, the LRE. Students must be provided with all the supports (including behavior supports) necessary to make this a successful educational experience.

BERNIE

When, even with appropriate assistance, students cannot behave in a way that allows them and their classmates to learn, they can be moved to a learning environment that is more appropriate. The following example illustrates the procedures that are used to ensure that these FAPE and LRE requirements are met.

Bernie is a seventh grade student who has an intellectual disability. His IEP team has determined that due to his mental and behavioral needs, a self-contained classroom is the best placement for him. To provide him with the most possible interactions with students without disabilities, his IEP specifies that he will eat lunch with a general education seventh grade class.

Bernie is delivered to his general education classroom by the instructional assistant each day and does well lining up with the other students and walking to the lunchroom. However, the loud lunchroom causes him stress, he is confused by the different serving lines, and he has trouble making himself understood when indicating his choices to the cafeteria workers. Most of his classmates are helpful, but some of them take pleasure in teasing him.

One day Bernie becomes very agitated by the teasing after going through the line. He grabs a student's tray and pushes him to the floor. The student hits his arm on a chair.

The immediate reaction of the teachers and administrators might be that Bernie is a danger and that he should be suspended from school. However, several requirements of IDEA must be followed to be sure that all aspects of the incident are carefully examined (see figure 8.1).

MANIFESTATION DETERMINATION

Bernie's IEP team, which includes his mother, teachers, and an administrator, meet to look at the situation, and at the effect that his disability has on his behavior in the lunchroom. The goal of the effort is to determine whether or not Bernie's actions are a manifestation of his disability — whether what he did was caused by his intellectual delays. The group examines his evaluation reports and talks to Bernie, his teacher, teacher assistant, and the students and teachers who observed the incident. See figure 8.2 for the form used.

They conclude that the behavior was caused by his disability. Due to his intellectual deficits, he was unable to understand the rules of the lunchroom, communicate effectively, and anticipate the consequences of his behavior once he became upset. Because there was a connection between the behavior and the disability, the school could not suspend or expel Bernie. He could not be punished for something that was essentially not his fault.

Bernie's case is an example of a situation in which the behavior is a manifestation of the disability. An example of no manifestation might be Len, a student with math learning disability, who calls in a bomb threat to the school. In Bernie's case he cannot be suspended, but Len can be

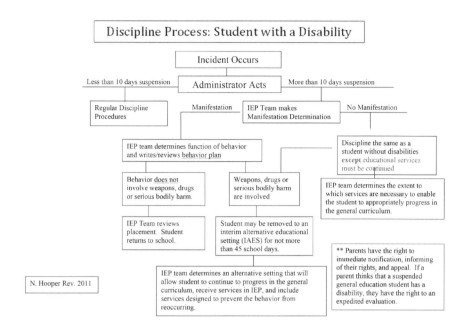

Figure 8.1. Discipline Process: Students with a Disability

treated as any other student regarding discipline procedures with one exception: the school division must continue to educate him. He can be suspended, but arrangements must be made for home-bound instruction or instruction in an alternate setting.

Further Steps

So what could be done with Bernie? Must the school just put up with Bernie hurting other students? Requiring Bernie to eat in his classroom instead of in the lunchroom is considered a change of placement, which must be agreed to by his IEP team. So once they completed the manifestation determination (MD), Bernie's team considered several options.

They consider having Bernie eat in his classroom for the rest of the year or sending the instructional assistant with him to the lunchroom each day, but they decide that they really want him to be able to interact with the seventh grade students on his own. So they write an addendum to the IEP stating that he would eat lunch in his classroom for one month. Meanwhile, they attend to two more requirements of IDEA to ensure that when he returned to the lunchroom he would no longer have anger outbursts. These requirements are the Functional Behavioral Assessment (FBA) and Behavior Intervention Plan (BIP) (see figure 8.3).

Student Name:

Student's Disability:

Proposed Discipline:

Offense:

Review:

    1. All relevant information in the student's fine, including:

          a. The IEP

          a. Any teacher observations

          a. Information provided by the parent(s):

    4. Determination:

Agree	Disagree	
		The conduct was a manifestation of the student's disability.
		The conduct was a direct result of the school division's failure to implement the student's IEP.
		The conduct is not a manifestation of the student's disability (both previous answers are "disagree")
		Determine if an FBA should be conducted and a BIP developed or a previous BIP reviewed. Yes ☐ No ☐
		The conduct was a manifestation of the student's disability (one or both of the first two answers are "agree". An FBA must be conducted and a BIP developed or a previous BIP reviewed.

Rationale:

Participant signatures:

Figure 8.2.   Manifestation Determination Review

Functional Behavioral Assessment and Behavior Intervention Plan

Bernie's IEP team meets twice to complete the FBA and BIP. In the first meeting they define the behavior very concretely (step 1). They might have stated it in these terms: "Bernie becomes agitated in the lunchroom and on one occasion lost control to the extent that he hurt another student."

Step 2 involves gathering information about the behavior. Some of the information, such as records review and interviews, was done as part of

Student: Billy Young

Steps 1-5 of the Functional Behavioral Assessment have been completed.

Restatement of Hypothesis regarding the function of the behavior:

The function of Billy's behavior is avoidance of assigned work and of structured interactions with other students. His lack of both academic and social skills cause him frustration and embarrassment when these weaknesses are made evident.

Replacement Behaviors:

Billy will complete assigned work.
Billy will play cooperatively with other students in his class.

The Plan: What supports will be in place in class or other environments to promote student success? What will be implemented to teach and monitor replacement behaviors? What adult responses be when student engages in the in appropriate behaviors? What will adult responses be when student engages in replacement behavior?

Plan	Person Responsible for training/monitoring
Billy will receive one hour per day of intensive reading and writing tutoring	Mr. Lawler
Billy will complete modified class assignments	Mrs. George
Billy will receive two hours per week of social skills training	Mrs. Pope
Billy will play cooperatively at least three times per day	Mrs. George

Student reinforcers: What types of reinforcers will be used to motivate learning and generalization of replacement behaviors?

When Billy completes each assignment he will get a work sticker. When 10 stickers are earned, he will get a prize.	Mrs. George
When Billy plays cooperatively with other students he will get a play sticker. When 10 stickers are earned, he will receive a prize	Mrs. George

Figure 8.3.

the MD process. The team decides that they want to know more, so they ask the school psychologist to observe Bernie in the lunchroom and also in his classroom. She agrees to take some data during her observations, such as counting the number of times Bernie exhibits agitated behavior. In addition, they want to interview Bernie's parents and the lunchroom workers. They agree to meet for their second meeting in one week.

At the second meeting the team completes step 3: determining the function of the behavior, or finding out why he did what he did. The information the team gathered helps them to see that Bernie is lacking the skills he needs to have a successful experience in the lunchroom. He is unable to focus his attention in the crowded, loud environment; he is not sure of the procedures for lining up and getting his food; and his speech is too difficult for the cafeteria workers to understand.

Step 4 is the development of a plan that will teach Bernie the skills he needs and support him as he learns to use them. Their plan includes having the teacher or assistant work with him in the empty lunchroom, modeling and practicing the procedures. They will also train two general education students to be his buddies in the lunchroom and develop a way for him to indicate his choices that is consistent with his communication capabilities. Once the team is confident that he is ready, Bernie will return to the lunchroom on a trial basis. After he exhibits success, his IEP will be amended again to indicate that he will spend each lunch period with the general education seventh grade students.

Steps 5 (implement the plan) and 6 (monitor the plan) are essential ones that are often neglected. Each person must complete the training tasks they agreed to in the plan, and one person must be responsible for continually determining how well the plan is working. If there are problems, the plan needs to be revised.

Other Legal Issues

Bernie and Len are examples of severe behaviors that would merit a long-term suspension or expulsion. However, in many cases students with disabilities misbehave in more minor ways such as being late to class, talking back to a teacher, and so on. These might normally result in two or three days of suspension, and as long as the total number of days is less than ten, the students can be disciplined like any other student. However, if the number of suspension days for behaviors that follow a common pattern reaches ten, then the requirements for MD, FBA, and BIP take effect.

There is a provision in the law for behaviors that constitute a danger to others, such as bringing a weapon to school, knowingly possessing illegal drugs, or inflicting serious bodily harm on someone. In that case, the school can remove the student to a temporary placement Interim Alternative Educational Setting (IAES) regardless of whether or not the behavior is a manifestation of the disability. The IEP team determines the location of the temporary placement (see figure 8.3).

Finally, it is important to understand that all students, particularly those with disabilities, require instruction and practice in how to behave in school. Many schools carefully monitor the number of days of suspension received by students with disabilities and develop BIPs once that number reaches six or seven. This proactive approach, while not required by law, assures that students who are experiencing difficulty following the rules are supported as they learn new behaviors. The implementation of the FBA and BIP process is by no means limited to students with disabilities. The Positive Behavior Intervention and Support program is a schoolwide system that recognizes the need for consistency, support, and instruction in the area of behavior for all students.

Websites

Disciplining students with disabilities from the legal perspective: http://www.wrightslaw.com/info/discipline.stud.dis.dwyer.pdf.

Alternate special education discipline flowchart: http://www.k12.wa.
us/SpecialEd/Families/pubdocs/SpEd_DisciplineFlowchart.pdf.

A clear explanation of the special education discipline procedures:
http://www.understandingspecialeducation.com/school-
discipline.html.

Least Restrictive Environment, Inclusion, and Mainstreaming: http://
www.twu.edu/inspire/least-restrictive.asp.

Behavioral and Emotional Disorders: http://specialed.about.com/od/
behavioremotiona1/a/Behavioral-And-Emotional-Disorders-In-
Special-Education.htm.

IRIS Module: Addressing Disruptive and Noncompliant Behaviors:
http://iris.peabody.vanderbilt.edu/module/bi1/.

CASE 15: WHERE DOES BILLY BELONG?

Mrs. George had her second grade classroom running smoothly by November. She had practiced behaviors and routines with her students, and
by now the students were able to work collaboratively and independently within the structures she had established. Her assessments showed
that they were making good academic progress.

She was not thrilled when Mr. Robinson, the principal, told her that
she was getting a new student. He said that Billy's family had moved into
the subsidized apartments nearby and that the school had not received
any records on him yet. When she registered him, his mother did not
indicate that he had had any problems in his previous school.

While it is never easy to get a new student in the middle of the school
year, Mrs. George was encouraged when she saw Billy. He was small for
his age, with a narrow face and short dark hair. He wore clean jeans and a
long-sleeved shirt and seemed subdued. She showed him his desk, but
made a note to herself to get him a smaller one that would enable him to
write more comfortably.

On his first day, Billy mostly watched the other students. When they
spoke to him he sometimes ignored them and other times answered with
one or two words. He did not complete any of the work that was assigned, nor did he pick up any books to read. Mrs. George was not
concerned at first, believing that he would settle into the work routine as
he became more comfortable.

By the second week, though, she realized that he had still completed
almost no work. He quietly resisted all of her attempts to get him started
on reading and writing activities, although he would sometimes write the
answers to math problems. In addition, he had started to move around
the room without permission, touching the desks and materials of other
students, making quiet comments to them, and distracting them from

their work in other ways. On the playground he joined in the games, but often the activities that included him ended in arguments or even fights.

When she spoke to him about his behavior and lack of work, he either ignored her or mumbled under his breath, and continued on with what he was doing. Mrs. George's calm, productive classroom atmosphere had somehow unraveled since the arrival of Billy. She was confused and frustrated. She liked Billy—he seemed vulnerable and needy, and he showed occasional signs of creativity and intelligence, but he was certainly a problem for her.

At the end of that week she received Billy's records from his previous school. She was not surprised to learn that he had been evaluated and identified as having an emotional disability. The evaluation indicated that his overall ability was above average, his math achievement was in the average range, and that his reading and writing skills were significantly below average.

His previous school had written an IEP specifying resource services to help him with his behavior issues. In some ways, Mrs. George was relieved. She had never taught a student like Billy before and knew she needed some help in figuring out how to get him to change his behavior and begin to learn. She sought out Mr. Lawler, the special education resource teacher.

Mr. Lawler had just reviewed Billy's records too, and Mrs. George filled him in on his behavior in her class. They made an initial plan. Mr. Lawler would observe Billy in his classroom and also bring him to the resource room to talk to him and do some initial assessments. He would also contact Billy's mother to find out more about his history and work with her to develop a transfer IEP.

Mr. Lawler's efforts were only partially successful. He noted Billy's erratic, avoidant behavior in his classroom and found out little from his conversation with Billy since he refused to talk about his home circumstances or his feelings about school. They did work together on some basic assessments, which revealed that Billy's reading skills were significantly delayed.

Billy's mother did not respond to any of Mr. Lawler's attempts to contact her. When he stopped by her apartment, no one answered the door. Finally, she did sign the transfer IEP that he sent home in Billy's backpack. The IEP specified one hour of daily resource room services, with goals related to behavior and reading.

But things in Mrs. George classroom were not improving. In fact, Billy was becoming bolder in his disruptive behaviors. He was never loud, but his wandering, quiet teasing, and refusal to complete any work were having a negative effect on his classmates. They were on edge much of the time, wondering what Billy would do next.

Mrs. George had tried applying her classroom behavior system on Billy, but the time outs, referrals to the office, and calls home (his mother never answered the phone) were totally ineffective. She spoke to the principal and to Mr. Lawler, hoping that since he had a label of emotional disturbance, he would be moved to a class for students with this disability.

Mr. Lawler indicated that before they took this step of changing Billy's placement to one that is more restrictive, they should try conducting a FBA and implementing a BIP. His IEP team was convened (without his mother, who did not respond to invitations or notices).

At the first meeting they reviewed the available data such as his records from his previous school, Mr. Lawler's observation and testing, Mrs. George's observations, and the few work samples he completed. They decided that Mrs. Lawler would speak with his general and special education teachers from his previous school and that Mrs. Pope, the guidance counselor, would spend time talking with Billy about his experiences and feelings. Once these data were collected, they would meet again to determine the function of his behaviors and develop a plan to help him learn more appropriate ways to interact at school.

Mr. Lawler gained some useful information from the staff at Billy's previous school. Billy's family (his mother, father, and brother) had spent time in the homeless shelter when they first arrived in that town, but then were able to move into an apartment. Within a year, however, the parents separated, and Billy left to live with his mother in the new city.

They said that he had an extremely difficult time settling into his kindergarten class: refusing to sit down, play with other children, or follow any teacher directions. For this reason, he was determined to have an emotional disability. They noted his reading weaknesses, but believed that the emotional issue was the primary problem.

Mrs. Pope spent a considerable amount of time with Billy: eating lunch with him, letting him do puzzles in her office while she worked, and watching him on the playground. She also included him in activities that she conducted with other children. He told her that he hated school, that he was ashamed of his attempts to read and write since they were so inferior, and that he was basically afraid of the other students. She came to see that he had very little idea of how to interact with adults, and concluded that his home life provided him with few models of appropriate behavior.

At the second meeting, the IEP team spent time discussing the function of Billy's behaviors—why did he behave as he did? They concluded that he was avoiding doing work that was difficult for him, but he was also seeking attention through his teasing of other students. It was clear to them that he needed intensive teaching in both reading and how to establish relationships with other people.

They also discussed ways in which to motivate Billy to change his behavior. Since his current actions were quite successful in enabling him to avoid engaging in work that was hard for him, he needed a strong incentive to learn and implement new behaviors. A further discussion involved setting methods to determine the success of the plan and scheduling a follow-up meeting. Based on these discussions, a BIP was developed (see figure 8.3).

Although Mrs. George was involved in the development of the plan, once it was in place she continued to be frustrated with Billy's behavior. She wanted Billy to be like the rest of her students and she didn't really think that it was fair to give him so much extra attention and other rewards for just following the classroom rules. She tried for a few weeks, but gradually stopped responding to his small behavior improvements.

Mr. Lawler became involved in other meetings and student emergencies and also neglected to provide the structure and consequences described in the plan. Billy, who had made some slight improvements, returned to his avoidant, disengaged actions. When the follow-up meeting was held, it was decided that a change in Billy's IEP was necessary. He was moved to a self-contained class for students with emotional disabilities in another school.

Questions to Ponder

1. Do you agree with the IEP team's decision to keep Billy in the general education class at the beginning of the case? Why or why not?
2. How much should Billy's effect on other students be a factor in this decision?
3. Was Billy's FBA and BIP appropriate? If not, what elements need to be changed and why?
4. What parts of the BIP contributed to its lack of success?
5. Do you think that Billy will be more successful in a self-contained education classroom? Why? What will need to be a part of the program for him to be successful? Do you think he could have met success in a different general education classroom or school?

Activities to Complete

1. Locate the forms and directions for the FBA and BIP process in your state or school division.
2. Use the form to rewrite Billy's BIP so that it is more likely to be followed by his teachers.
3. Observe a classroom for students with emotional disabilities. How is it structured? What behavior procedures are in place? Are they effective? What would you do differently? What are the characteristics of some of the students?

4. Continue this case, describing what happens when Billy goes to a self-contained education classroom. Write it with two endings — one that is unsuccessful and one that is successful.

CASE 16: CAN MICHAEL CONTROL HIMSELF?

Mrs. Black was frustrated with the school, as usual. Yesterday she got a call from the assistant principal telling her that Michael had been suspended again, this time for five days. When Michael entered middle school in September, the IEP team had assured her that they had good services in place to address his ADHD. They assured her that he would not be getting suspended as often as he had been in elementary school. But here it was only November and he was being suspended for the third time.

Michael was diagnosed with ADHD when he was in preschool. He is a good-looking, engaging child who likes to have a fun time. He enjoys working with his father, who is a contractor, and he can make anything with his hands. He has never liked school, though, as he has a very difficult time sitting still, attending, and completing assignments.

He began taking medication for ADHD in kindergarten and it works well when he takes it consistently. But Michael complains that it makes his stomach hurt and decreases his appetite. He avoids taking it whenever he can. He was identified as being eligible for special education under the Other Health Impaired category at the end of his kindergarten year.

Everyone likes Michael. He has an infectious smile and relates well to people. Mrs. Black loves his high energy level — it is similar to her husband's, and their household is never dull. They are always working on projects, engaging in sports activities, fishing or hunting outdoors, and finding other ways to stay active. Reading, quiet conversation, or even spending time on the computer are not part of their home routine.

All of the problems relating to Michael occur at school. His grades are low due to missed work and poor study skills. His reading and math levels are average, but he takes a long time to complete any assignment, and nothing is ever done without an adult standing by him to keep him on task.

His seventh grade IEP states that the inclusion teacher will be in his general education math class each day, and that Michael will attend a resource class daily. The goal of the resource class is to keep him caught up on all of his assignments. At this point in the school year the program is working relatively well.

Michael often neglects to bring his assignments and books to resource class, but the special education teacher stays in touch with his special education teachers and makes sure that he completes most of his assignments. The problems occur during unstructured class times and outside of classes.

It seems as though Michael looks for ways to make mischief. He has never hurt anyone, but he is a specialist in setting up pranks and playing tricks on people. In September he was suspended for four days for pouring liquid glue on the chairs before several students sat in them. Today's call came after he put a plastic snake on a girl's shoulder, causing her to scream and nearly faint. When Mrs. Black went to the school to pick up Michael she spoke to Mr. Morrow, his English teacher.

"I am so frustrated with Michael," Mr. Morrow said. "He appears to have no self-control whatsoever! If he thinks of something to do that will get everyone riled up, he will do it regardless of the consequences. I can't turn my back on him for one minute. He is too old to need constant supervision."

"Yes, that is part of his disability," Mrs. Black agreed. "It is the reason that he has an IEP. He cannot evaluate the results an action or restrain his impulses to so something interesting."

As Mrs. Black was leaving the school with Michael, Mrs. Gray, the assistant principal, stopped her and said that since this suspension would cause Michael's total days of suspension to reach more than ten, they would need to hold a MD meeting. Mrs. Black took Michael home and talked to him once again about controlling his impulses and taking his medication. He would have no computer or video game privileges while he was suspended.

At the MD meeting the following day, Michal's IEP team met. In attendance were:

Mrs. Black, mother
Ms. Pollock, special education teacher
Mr. Morrow, general education English teacher
Mrs. Gray, assistant principal
Mrs. Little, school psychologist

They reviewed his records and discussed the circumstances of the incident.

Mr. Morrow opened the discussion. "I think that Michael can control his behavior. He just likes all the attention that he gets when he pulls these stunts. If we quit babying him and apply consistent consequences like suspension, he will start to think before he acts."

Ms. Pollock noted that he is much better when he takes his medication, but that he sometimes refuses it or hides it in his mouth and later spits it out. Mrs. Black said that they often had issues at home with his medication as well, and that she does not ask him to take it on weekends and vacation days. He really does not like the way it makes him feel.

"As I said to Mr. Morrow," Mrs. Black continued, "Michael's action was a manifestation of his disability. His ADHD makes him unable to stop himself from doing something that he thinks is interesting or exciting. I think that it is the responsibility of the school to arrange close supervision so that these things don't happen. Suspension is not really a punishment for him, even though I take away all his privileges. School is very stressful for him and he likes being home. More suspensions will not change his behavior."

Questions to Ponder

1. What should be done about Michael's reluctance to take his medication?
2. What do you think of Michael's mother's beliefs about her son's behavior? Do you think he would act better if she had a different attitude?
3. Did the school follow Michael's IEP? If so, how should it be rewritten so that Michael does not continue to get in trouble?
4. Do you think that Michael's ADHD will continue to cause him difficulty when he is an adult and no longer has to attend school? Why or why not?

Activities to Complete

1. Role play Michael's IEP meeting, with someone taking the part as each of the participants. Complete the form in the introduction to this chapter when you complete your discussion. Be sure to describe the rationale for your decision.
2. If you decide that the incident is not a manifestation of his disability, what consequences should be arranged for Michael? What are the benefits and drawbacks of suspension?
3. If you decide that the incident is a manifestation of his disability, what should the team do to ensure that he does not terrify a classmate again? What should be included in a new BIP?

Resources

Handling a Manifestation Determination Review: http://www.wrightslaw.com/info/discipl.mdr.strategy.htm

Information on various behavior topics, including MD:http://www.doe.sd.gov/oess/sped-pbis.aspx

Discipline process flow chart:http://www.esc7.net/users/0037/docs/behdisciplineflowchart07.pdf

NINE

Assessment

Assessment is an important part of education, and we use it all the time. However, we often use it automatically and sometimes blindly, making inadequate or wrong use of the information that assessments yield. Assessment that is well planned and well used is extremely powerful, and an essential part of educating all students.

DEFINITION

What is assessment? One way to define it is "the systematic collection of performance information for the purpose of making decisions." It is helpful to look at each part of that definition for a more thorough understanding.

Systematic means that the assessment instrument has reliability (it is consistent, measuring the same thing each time it is used) and validity (it measures what it says it measures). For example, we might want to know how familiar young children are with the alphabet. We don't have time to ask them to identify all of the twenty-six letters, so we decide to select only five letters. On test 1 we ask one set of students to identify A, B, C, and X. On test 2 we choose Y, W, F, and G as the stimulus letters for another set of students.

Not surprisingly, students who took test 1 scored much better than the students who took test 2. Neither test is valid, as it is not an indication of a child's knowledge of the entire alphabet. According to test 1, they know the alphabet well, but according to test 2 they have little knowledge. Both tests may be reliable, getting similar results every time, but they are not valid.

The results might be unreliable if the test is administered in the school by a strange school adult in one case and by the child's mother at home in another case. Different results would be due to different testing circumstances rather than to different levels of child alphabet knowledge.

While the previous example may seem extreme, it is not at all uncommon for teachers to give a test that is not measuring what they think it is measuring. A social studies unit test consisting of multiple choice and essay questions may be measuring reading and writing abilities as much as it is measuring knowledge of the Civil War. In fact, a student with a reading and writing disability may know the Civil War information very well and still fail the test.

The *performance information* collected can take many forms (see figure 9.1). It can vary in purpose (formative or summative), in method of performance (written, oral, behavioral), in type of written answer (multiple choice, essay, short answer), in type of data collected (observational checklist, frequency or duration behavioral data collection), in test setting (group or individual), and in source of the assessment (external or self).

The *decisions* that are determined by the tests will vary as well. The results may determine placement (in reading groups, gifted or special education programs), grades, instructional changes, learning objective changes, or behavior management plans.

Take a minute to think about assessment in your classroom or a classroom you have visited.

Purpose	Formative	Given as instruction is ongoing. Used to inform instructional changes
	Summative	Given after instruction is completed on a topic. Used to determine grades, promotion, entry to certain programs, etc.
Type of performance required	Written	Hand written or computer based; multiple choice, essay, short answer, matching
	Oral	Individual or group
	Behavioral	Examples: completing a project, acting out an answer, demonstrating a concept
Test setting	Large group	Requires ability to concentrate despite surrounding activity
	Small group	Can be useful if tests are to be read aloud
	Individual	For certain norm-referenced tests and oral responses
Source of assessment	External	Teacher, peer, state-mandated test
	Internal	Self-assessment

Figure 9.1.   Aspects of Assessment

1. Why are you giving the test?
2. What are you testing?
3. What will you do with the results?

Likely answers may be that you are giving the test because you reached the end of a chapter, that you are testing students' knowledge of the chapter information, and that you will put the grades in your grade book. If that is true, then you might need to look more closely, asking questions such as:

Does the test really measure student understanding of the most important concepts in the chapter?

Will students in your class be able to show their knowledge on this test?

What will you do if some students perform poorly?

Can you use the results to make changes in the way that you teach?

CLASSROOM DATA COLLECTION

This chapter will focus on using assessment wisely to improve instruction for all students, especially those with learning and behavior challenges. Consistent use of classroom data collection such as Curriculum-Based Measurement (CBM) and behavior monitoring ensures that instructional and management decisions are well made. Designing tests that measure what you think they are measuring and that incorporate IEP mandated accommodations ensures that your tests give you accurate information about student performance.

Curriculum-Based Measurement

Marianne was a thoughtful, seasoned fourth grade teacher. She had a well-organized classroom and knew how to keep her instruction stimulating for her students. Her assessments took the form of chapter and unit tests, writing samples, and weekly spelling tests. When students did well on the tests she believed that she had taught well. But each year she had some students who did not achieve As or Bs on the tests, possibly because they had difficulties with basic reading or math skills. Her assessments told her nothing about their actual academic needs.

This past summer Marianne read two articles on CBM and she thought that this form of progress monitoring might enable her to teach all of her students more effectively. She consulted the special education teacher at the beginning of the school year and together they designed progress monitoring assessments in the areas of reading and math. She administered the math CBM to the whole class as a group each Monday, and gave individual reading CBMs to the five students who struggled most in reading.

Marianne felt that the change in her teaching was significant. She now knew exactly which reading and math areas needed extra work and was able to direct her instruction to those specific areas. In addition, she could see the results of her instruction each week. She did not need to wait for the results of chapter test, when it was often too late to reteach. She also appreciated the motivational aspect of the tests. Students loved seeing the graphed results when their scores rose, and participated in determining adjustments in methods and practice when progress stalled.

Developing CBM materials involves looking carefully at the curriculum. In the area of mathematics, you construct a test that includes examples of each type of problem a student will be expected to solve by the end of the school year. Make several versions of the test with random numerals and random locations of problems on the page. This can be administered to a group of students. Graph the number of digits written correctly.

Reading CBM tests may vary according to grade level. Elementary reading progress is accurately measured through fluency assessments. In these assessments students read aloud from a grade-level passage for one minute. The score is the number of words read correctly. In middle and secondary levels, Maze passages are a better measure. To develop this assessment, select a grade-level passage and delete every seventh word. For the missing word, supply three choices (see figure 9.2). As the student reads for two and a half minutes, she selects the correct word. The score is the number of words replaced correctly.

As knowledge and skills grow through the year, students' scores increase. Stalled progress can be addressed immediately. While the development and administration of CBM measures may seem to be complicated and time consuming, the information it yields can improve instruction significantly. An essential component of this improvement is teacher ex-

Directions: the student reads the passage aloud, selecting the correct word from the choices. From The Most Dangerous Game by Richard Connell

Rainsford sprang up and moved quickly to the rail, mystified. He strained his eyes in the *(direction, punctually, regularly)* from which the reports had come, *(linen, silver, but)* it was like trying to see *(through, saw, fluffy)* a blanket. He leaped upon the *(fowl, rail, nerve)* and balanced himself there to get *(greater, insect, taste)* elevation. His pipe, striking a rope, *(was, crooked, rotten)* knocked from his mouth. He lunged *(property, for, connect)* it. A short, hoarse cry came *(from, mine, reflect)* his lips as he realized he *(minus, tray, had)* reached too far and had lost *(nervously, whose, his)* balance. The cry was pinched off *(short, wonderful, dog)* as the blood-warm waters of the *(Caribbean, someone, reject)* Sea closed over his head.

Figure 9.2.   Example of a Maze Test

amination of the CBM results each week, and adjustment of instruction based on this examination.

Behavior Monitoring

While we are comfortable with collecting information on student academic performance in the form of tests and other graded assignments, collecting data related to student behavior is less common. However, it can be very powerful, and a useful solution to nagging problems.

Jonathan's first period English class was driving him crazy this year. He knew he had designed engaging lessons, and the students were doing the work, but they were so noisy! They called out answers, talked to each other, and generally kept the sound and energy level high all period. Jonathan felt worn out each day by the time second period began. He suspected that many of the students were also disturbed by the elevated noise level and would welcome a solution.

Jonathan needed to look more closely at what was happening in his class in a systematic way. Data collection is a way to do that. He could count certain behaviors (frequency), time how long a behavior lasts (duration), or use a rating scale to determine how strong a behavior is (intensity) (see figure 9.3).

Because he felt so overwhelmed by this group and was not sure what to measure, Jonathan asked the guidance counselor, Allison, to come observe. At the end of the day they reviewed her notes and saw that one of the basic problems was calling out without seeking permission to speak. Jonathan had always been casual about enforcing a hand-raising rule, but it had never been a problem in other classes. This group was different.

Counting the frequency of the call-outs seemed to be the way to begin to tackle the problem. Allison came in twice more to begin the frequency count. On the third day Jonathan did it himself by transferring a paper clip from his left pocket to his right each time he observed a call-out. After a week of data collection, he put the results on a graph and showed it to the class. They were all surprised to note that they called out an average of forty-seven times per day. Together they developed a procedure for asking permission before speaking.

The change was dramatic. Jonathan continued to count the call-outs and add the results to the graph on the wall, and the numbers dropped quickly. Without any other motivational system, the very fact that the behaviors were being counted and recorded caused the students to monitor and control their classroom communication. They continued the counting for three more weeks, when it became evident that it was no longer necessary. Both Jonathan and the students enjoyed the newly calm atmosphere in the first period English class.

Behavior Samples – data collected while the behavior is taking place	
Frequency – count the number of times a behavior is performed (while it is being done)	Count the number of times any student calls out without raising a hand. Count the number of times Mark compliments another student.
Duration – measure how long a behavior lasts	See how long Bart and Abe play together without arguing. Measure how long it takes Alison to complete a math paper.
Intensity – measure the strength of behavior	Use a rating scale to determine the intensity of John's outburst.
Data collected after behavior has occurred	
Permanent Product – count or measure something in the absence of the student	Count number of worksheets completed. Rate the cleanliness of the classroom at the end of each day
Locus – record where a behavior has occurred	Note the classes and areas in the school in which Oliver gets into trouble. Record the classes in which Gabriella completes all her work.

Figure 9.3. Data Collection

This example is not an uncommon one—frequently the collection of data on certain behaviors is enough to change the behavior. But often further interventions in the form of a behavior plan is necessary. Without the careful monitoring of the behavior, however, it is difficult to make any changes.

Graphing

As both of these examples illustrate, making the results of the classroom data collection in the form of a graph is an important part of this process. The graph serves several purposes:

1. Demonstrating effectiveness
2. Motivating
3. Communicating

When results of frequent academic or behavioral probes are displayed on graphs, the trends are clearly evident. Weekly reading measures may show that a student is not gaining in her ability to read fluently. Since the focus is on helping her catch up with her classmates, it is essential that a new instructional method be found that will cause her results to increase consistently. Continued probes will indicate whether or not the new method is working. This type of frequent, consistent classroom collection is a very powerful way to keep close tabs on studentS academic and behavioral progress.

Putting the results in graph form can also be motivating for both students and teachers. Rising results indicate that a method is working and also that the studentS and teacher are putting forth good effort. A resolution to keep the upward slope of the progress line may help to even increase those efforts.

Imagine bringing a graph that indicates improving reading scores or a higher percentage of papers turned in to a parent-teacher conference. It indicates a careful attention to student progress on the part of the teacher and gives gratification and confidence to the parent. The pictorial representation makes progress clear to everyone.

TEST ACCESSIBILITY

While classroom data collection is an important part of instruction, we still use traditional tests to measure student skills and knowledge. A well-designed test can be answered by everyone, including students who have reading, reasoning, or organizational difficulties.

A test that is accessible will have questions that are at the appropriate reading level and use only the essential words. Important information might be in bold font. It is important that the wording is in a positive form, asking a student to give a correct answer rather than selecting an incorrect answer. Examples of directly worded questions are given in figure 9.4.

Item choices should also be direct and about equal in length. The pages will not be cluttered. If visuals are used, they should be clear and have labels if appropriate. Color and good visual contrast are important. Examine your test to be sure it does not require knowledge or skills that are not relevant to the topic being evaluated

TEST ACCOMMODATIONS

You may have students in your classroom who have disabilities that affect their ability to show what they know on tests that you give. In these cases, the students will have IEPs that specify accommodations related to classroom and statewide assessments. The accommodations may affect the timing of the test, setting, presentation or response (see figure 9.5).

If there is a testing accommodation in the IEP, it is because the IEP team has determined that the student requires this variation in order to show what he knows of the subject. He needs the accommodation on every test that is given throughout the school year, not only on the end of year state assessment. You as the teacher are legally bound by the IEP to

Examples of Test Questions that have been modified through the use of simplified language, clear "question" words, and active voice.

1. Original question:

The atmospheric condition in which air currents circulate at extremely high velocities in a limited area is called a _____.

Modified question:

What do you call a very fast wind that is moving in a small circle?

2. Original question:

Describe the rationale behind the southern states making good their threat of disunion of 1860.

Modified question:

Why did the southern states decide to leave the union in 1860?

Figure 9.4.   Modified Test Questions

provide this accommodation consistently. It is not meant to give the student an unfair advantage, but to allow him the same access to the test that students without disabilities have.

You would not consider asking a blind student to take a printed test without supplying a Braille version or administering it orally. Nor should you ask a student with attention deficit disorder (ADD) to take a test in a large noisy group even though his IEP specifies a small group setting. In each case the disability blocks accessibility to the test without the accommodation.

Similarly, it is essential that the student use the accommodation consistently so that she is familiar taking the test under those conditions. For example, if a student is required by the IEP to dictate to a scribe on the state end-of-year test, she must be practicing this procedure throughout the year. She must learn how to organize her thoughts mentally and specify all aspects of the written product to the scribe, such as punctuation marks and capital letters.

This does not mean that you as a teacher cannot work with the student to improve to a point at which she might no longer need the accommodation. Perhaps with your help the student is gaining new reading comprehension skills. As she begins to do grade-level work, you determine that he might take your tests in the written form even though oral administration is listed in his IEP. The procedure in this case would be to have him take some practice tests in the standard form while graded tests are still administered orally. When he seems ready, you gather the IEP team and make an official change to the IEP deleting that specific testing accommodation.

Presentation	Oral reading (tape or adult)
	Large print
	Magnification devices
	Sign language
	Braille
	Tactile graphics
	Manipulatives
	Audio amplification devices
	Screen reader
Response	Using a computer or a scribe to record answers (directly or through a tape recorder)
	Using an augmentative communication device or other assistive technology
	Using a Brailler
	Responding directly in the test booklet rather than on an answer sheet
	Using organizational devices including calculation devices, spelling and grammar assistive devices, or graphic organizers.
Setting	Administering the test to the student alone
	Testing in a separate room
	Testing in a small group
	Adjusting the lighting
	Providing noise buffers (headphones, earplugs
Scheduling	Extended time
	Multiple or frequent breaks
	Change in testing schedule or order of subjects
	Testing over multiple days

Figure 9.5.   Typical Test Accommodations

ALTERNATE ASSESSMENT

We do not have to be locked into traditional summative tests such as those given at the end of the chapter or semester. Even formative tests such as CBM are only one of many possible methods. Just as students have many different ways of learning, they have many different ways of expressing what they know. UDL states that students should have multiple means of expressing what they know. Written tests are only one possibility for this expression.

Authentic Assessment gives students a chance to demonstrate an understanding of information through the completion of projects. Often these projects integrate several different aspects of a subject or even different subject areas. Some examples of authentic assessments:

1. How much trash do you produce in a day? Collect all of the trash you produce in a twenty-four-hour period. Organize the trash into categories, report the environmental problems with each type of trash, and come up with possible solutions for these problems. Use the information to devise an advertising campaign to increase public awareness about the problem of waste disposal.
2. Become familiar with Native American legends. Write your own legend explaining how something came to be. Your work will be

submitted for publication for the fourth grade Indian Legend Book in the School Library.

3. You have been asked to plan a meal for all eighty-five members of the Bulls' team. Select a recipe for an appetizer, entrée, and dessert. Show the original recipe, and then write directions for cooking the meal for eighty-five people. In addition, develop a shopping list that includes likely prices for each item.

Each of these assessments requires students to conduct research and use the research to create a product that could actually be used. A rubric would be included with the assignment, but part of the assessment is whether or not the final product fills a function—if the ad campaign really will increase waste disposal awareness or if the legend is one that future students will select to read in the library.

Such assessments not only motivate students who are bored or intimidated by written tests, but also challenge them to integrate their knowledge and to work collaboratively, drawing on different strengths in each other. Ideally, several possible projects would be presented and students would be able to choose which assignment best fits their interests and strengths.

Self-assessment is an extremely powerful tool that both students and teachers can be trained to use. Some teachers use some form of exit ticket every day, asking students to perform a task taught that day and to rate their level of understanding. This exercise not only informs the teacher of the success of his lesson, but also promotes self-awareness in the students.

In the Stop Light exercise, students select either a green, yellow, or red sticky note, depending on their level of understanding. On a green note, they write what they learned that day. On a yellow note they write a question and on a red they indicate what stopped their learning that day. The notes are stuck in sections on the board and discussed.

Self-assessment on the part of teachers is just as important. Some type of system to promote reflection is most useful, such as a box to be filled in next to each day's lesson plan, a reflective journal completed at the end of a day, or an oral summary of the day recorded on the drive home. Topics to include in the reflection might be what worked in a lesson and why, what you would do differently when you teach the lesson again and why, and what data you need to make an informed decision about a problem you are facing.

Assessment is an essential part of teaching and learning. It gives us an awareness of the current state of learning so that we can move forward and continue to grow. Careful, consistent use of assessment is particularly important for students who are academic or behavioral delayed since it gives us a clear indication of the results of our efforts to help them make speedy progress.

Websites

> Webinars and other training programs related to student progress monitoring: http://www.studentprogress.org/library/Webinars.asp #ABC.
> Modules that illustrate different forms of assessment: http://iris.peabody.vanderbilt.edu/iris-resource-locator/.
> Test Accessibility Modification Inventory: http://peabody.vanderbilt.edu/docs/pdf/PRO/TAMI_Technical_Manual.pdf.
> Many resources related to CBM, including a Maze generator: http://www.interventioncentral.org/teaching-resources/downloads.
> A good example of the use of a math CBM: http://www.studentprogress.org/library/CaseStudy/math_grade3.pdf.

CASE 17: HOW CAN ASSESSMENT HELP MARCUS?

Mr. Hudson was in his second year of teaching third grade. His first year was a learning year, and he knew he could have done many things better, but he received positive, encouraging reviews from his principal. He loved being in his second year, when he knew the routines and the pitfalls and could concentrate on being a good teacher.

Now, in November, most of his students were progressing well. They followed the classroom procedures, completed their work, and cooperated with each other. They appeared to be learning, as they generally scored well on the weekly spelling tests and chapter tests that he gave. But Mr. Hudson was concerned about two students in particular.

Courtney

Courtney said that she hated math. She seemed to pay attention when new concepts were introduced, but was continually confused when independent practice was assigned. She resisted starting any math work, often did not complete papers, and scored low on all math tests. Mr. Hudson had tried working individually with her on basic concepts and assigned her a math buddy to help her with work completion. But nothing seemed to be working.

Mr. Hudson decided to consult with the math specialist, Ms. Rose, to get some new techniques to use with Courtney. Ms. Rose looked at some of Courtney's work and test scores. She also talked with Courtney about her frustrations with math.

Then she talked with Mr. Hudson about CBM. She said that if Mr. Hudson was going to help Courtney make progress, he first needed to know exactly where the starting point was—exactly what Courtney could and could not do in math. He then needed to develop a way to track her progress as they worked together on her weak areas. He needed to develop and administer some assessments.

So, with Ms. Rose's help, Mr. Hudson developed a CBM based on his third grade curriculum. It included one or two problems for each of the third grade concepts such as place value, reading graphs, fractions, addition, subtraction, multiplication, division, and problems calling for application of these concepts. They decided to administer the test to all of his students to see where everyone stood in math.

The results indicated that, while Courtney was by far the weakest student (she solved only 25 percent of the problems correctly), some other students were confused by specific concepts. Few of the students scored 100 percent since the test consisted of skills that had not yet been taught. Mr. Hudson decided that he would continue to give a version of the same test every two weeks as a way to monitor the math progress of each of the students in his class.

But Courtney needed even more direct monitoring. After analyzing the results of her CBM test, he determined that she lacked basic number sense. She missed such problems as:

1. Write these three numbers in order from smallest to largest:
2. 542, 97, 286, 4609
3. Place ‹, › or = between these numbers:

$$351\_\_\_\_380$$
$$2081\_\_\_\_2930$$

Since this was such a basic concept that formed the basis for many other math applications, Mr. Hudson decided to focus on this skill. He developed a set of mastery tests that evaluated this one skill and gave it to Courtney each week after they had practiced with number charts, games, and other manipulatives such as Cuisenaire rods. When she reached 90 percent mastery in the number sense area, Mr. Hudson moved on to addition and subtraction, using tests he developed to give them both clear information about Courtney's weekly progress.

Both Mr. Hudson and Courtney were encouraged by her progress. She loved watching the graphed scores rise each week. When the scores started to flatten out, she and Mr. Hudson both knew that they had to find new ways of learning and to work harder. For the first time in her school career, Courtney began to feel positive about math.

Mr. Hudson made good use of the progress monitoring CBM that all of his students took every two weeks. He analyzed the errors closely and was sure to focus on any concepts that were unclear to any of his students. He too felt that he was much more successful in his math teaching since he began to use CBM to inform his instruction.

Marcus

Marcus was a whiz at math. He aced nearly all of the biweekly math CBM tests. He loved math. But reading was a different story. He avoided reading whenever possible, preferring to be playing ball or solving math problems. When Mr. Hudson asked him to read aloud, Marcus read slowly, laboriously sounding out every word, even ones he had already read several times on the same page. He had difficulty with vowel sounds and consonant diagraphs. He seemed to read first grade books independently, but struggled when presented with second grade material.

Writing was also a struggle for Marcus. He loved to tell stories, but when asked to write them down he had difficulty getting even ten words on the page. His work was often difficult to read since most words were misspelled and his letters were poorly formed.

Questions to Ponder

1. How could Mr. Hudson use CBM to help Marcus with his reading development?
2. What skills should he assess?
3. Develop a third grade level fluency assessment for Marcus.
4. How could CBM help Marcus improve his writing?
5. Develop a third grade writing assessment for Marcus.
6. Imagine that, after working with Marcus, Mr. Hudson determines that he may have a learning disability. How would CBM data be helpful to the eligibility team in determining the presence or absence of this disability?
7. How could Mr. Hudson use exit cards to improve his teaching?

Activities to Complete

1. Look at the curriculum for a middle or secondary math course. Develop a math progress monitoring CBM for that course.
2. Develop a maze CBM for a sixth grade class.
3. Develop a set of test accommodations that Marcus would need in order to demonstrate what he knows in science and social studies. Describe why you chose each accommodation and how it could best be implemented.
4. Look at http://www.studentprogress.org/library/CaseStudy/math_grade3.pdf for an example of a third grade CBM. Develop an alternate form of the test.

CASE 18: IS THIS TEST FAIR?

At the beginning of the school year, Margaret, the special education teacher, came to talk with Robert about a student who would be in his eleventh grade history class.

Antoine was identified as having a learning disability when he was in third grade. He has average intelligence and average ability in math. However, he has dyslexia which limits his reading and writing abilities. He has received intensive instruction in self-contained settings but is still reading no higher than a seventh grade level.

More recently he had become more adept at using computer software to assist with reading and writing. Word prediction programs helped him to write much more clearly and correctly. Programs that read websites and material he had scanned into the computer enabled him to research and study more independently.

Because of these new skills, and his particular interest in history, his IEP team determined that he should be included in a general education history course. Margaret thought that he had a good chance of doing well in Robert's class with appropriate accommodations and modifications.

Margaret said that she would be collaborating with Robert throughout the year. She would come to the class session three times each week and would keep track of Antoine's progress. She talked with Robert about modifying the way he presented his material, using more visuals and hands-on activities. She noted that Antoine had testing accommodations listed in his IEP. He needed to have tests read aloud since he could not read eleventh grade material. He was also allowed to dictate answers to essay questions to a scribe.

Antoine was a very quiet member of the class for the first few weeks. He interacted well with the other students, but generally kept to himself. Robert had not thought very much about changing his teaching style for Antoine, thinking that Antoine's learning was really Margaret's problem. He used Power Point to make presentations of the history ideas and facts, relying on students to take notes. Students were also required to read the text each night.

In the second week Margaret asked to meet with Robert. She said that she had not yet been able to get the history text in audio form, or scan the book into the computer read-aloud program. For that reason, Antoine was struggling to read the daily assignments.

He was also unable to listen and write at the same time, so she would need to provide him with copies of the notes. She asked Robert to give her advance copies of the notes he planned to use for each lecture; she would make sure that Antoine used them. Robert did put copies of his notes in Margaret's box when he remembered, but he often forgot.

Periodically Robert engaged students in discussions about their interpretations of the history they were studying. When he did this in the third week of the semester, he was surprised when Antoine made a very thoughtful addition to the discussion. He had clearly been listening in class and understood the material.

In the fourth week Robert gave a test. Unfortunately, Margaret was in a meeting that day and could not attend the class. Robert handed the test to Antoine and he spent the class period marking answers and responding to the essay questions just like all of the other students. Surprisingly to Robert (but not to Margaret), Antoine failed the test. Many of his multiple choice answers were incorrect, and his essay answers were short and almost unreadable.

Many people were upset when the test results were returned. Robert knew that Antoine knew the facts and their implications so he could not understand why he got them wrong on the test. Margaret knew that Robert had violated Antoine's IEP, a serious infraction. Antoine was more upset than anyone. He loved the general education history class and was afraid that now he would be sent back to the self-contained class.

The incident caused Robert to think seriously about his teaching and assessment practices. He asked himself some basic questions: When he gave a test, what did he really want to measure? Reading and writing ability, or history knowledge?

He knew that the results would have been different if Margaret had been able to read the test to Antoine, but he wanted to find a way to examine Antoine's knowledge without the help of someone else. In addition, he saw that there were other students who did show all that they knew on his recent test.

How could he measure what his students know without having to give a written test?

Questions to Ponder

1. Think about Robert's first question. Discuss the relationship between reading and writing ability and assessments that are generally given.
2. How do you think that Antoine learned much of the history information without being able to read the textbook? What skills would he need to use to do this?
3. If you were Robert, how would you change the way you are teaching to meet the needs of a student who has a reading disability?
4. If Robert found a way to test Antoine without having someone read tests to him, what should be done about the accommodation in Antoine's IEP?

Activities to Complete

1. List alternate assessments that would work for Robert's eleventh grade history class.
2. For at least one of the items on the list, develop a sample assignment sheet, with specific directions and examples. Make it clear enough that students would follow it without further teacher explanation.
3. Write five history test items (multiple choice or short answer). Give two examples for each item—one that with unnecessarily complex language and one that follows the rules outlined in the introduction to this chapter.

Appendix A: List of Cases by Disability Area

Case	LD	ED	ASD	ID	HI	OHI
1	X	X				
2	X					
3	X					
4		X	X			
5			X			
6	X		X			
7			X			
8				X		
9	X	X				
10						
11			X			
12					X	
13						
14						X
15		X				
16						X
17	X					
18	X					

Appendix B: List of Cases by Grade Level

Case	K	1	2	3	4	5	6	7	8	9	10	11	12
1							X						
2										X			
3				X									
4									X				
5	X												
6													X
7				X									
8													X
9						X							
10					X								
11										X			
12									X				
13							X	X	X				
14	X												
15			X										
16								X					
17				X									
18												X	

111

References

Chaney, R. S. (2002). *Teaching children to care: Classroom management for ethical and academic growth, K–8*. Turners Falls, MA: Center for Responsive Schools.

Eisenberg, L. (1981, June). Leo Kanner, M. D. 1894–1981. *The American Journal of Psychiatry*, 138. Retrieved from http://www.ablongman.com/html. /productinfo/friend2e_MLS/0205505317ch04.pdf.

Friend, M. (2008). *Co-teach! A handbook for creating and sustaining effective classroom partnerships in inclusive schools*. Greensboro, NC: Author.

Linson, M. (2014). Smart classroom management: Simply effective tips and strategies. Retrieved from http://www.smartclassroommanagement.com/about-michael-linsin/.

McKeachie, M. J. (1999). *Teaching tips: Strategies, research, and theory for college and university teachers*. Boston: Houghton Mifflin.

RTI Action Network: A program of the National Center for Learning Disabilities. Retrieved from http://www.rtinetwork.org.

Teaching with case studies. (1994, Winter). *Speaking of Teaching: Stanford University Newsletter on Teaching*. Retrieved from https://web.stanford.edu/dept/CTL/cgi-bin/docs/newsletter/case_studies.pdf.

About the Authors

Dr. Roberta Gentry received her bachelor's degree in psychology from Mary Baldwin College in Virginia. She worked in psychiatric hospitals, as a neuropsychology test technician, and as a contracted school psychologist before returning to school to complete her master's degree. After completing her master's of teaching in general education and special education from the University of Virginia, she became a special education teacher, working as a grade-level chairperson, mentor coordinator, and lead teacher before serving as a district level administrator of special education.

Dr. Gentry earned her doctorate degree in special education disability policy and leadership from Virginia Commonwealth University. Currently, she is an assistant professor at the University of Mary Washington in Fredericksburg, Virginia. She teaches special education coursework, professional development courses, and supervises student teachers.

Dr. Norah Hooper has experience as both a general and special education teacher at the middle and elementary levels. She taught in inclusive settings for fifteen years. Additionally, she has served as a district-wide special education director and as a professor of special education at the University of Mary Washington. Dr. Hooper holds degrees in English literature and elementary and special education from St. Mary's College at Notre Dame, SUNY Cortland and UNC Chapel Hill. Her PhD in special education is from George Mason University.

Made in United States
Orlando, FL
17 December 2021

11854987R00079